*Yacoub & Tomás*

*For those trapped
between condemnation & blessing*

# UNCIRCUMCISED

WELCOMING LGBTQ PEOPLE INTO THE FAMILY OF GOD

© 2017, Brian John Karcher / Yacoub & Tomás
All rights reserved.

No part of this book may be used or reproduced by any means, graphic, electronic, or mechanical, including photocopying, recording, taping or by any information storage retrieval system without the written permission of the author /publisher except in the case of brief quotations embodied in critical articles and reviews.

The Bible quotations are from The Holy Bible, English Standard Version® (ESV®), copyright © 2001 by Crossway, a publishing ministry of Good News Publishers. Used by permission. All rights reserved.

*Contact Information*
**Brian John Karcher**
author | advocate | ally
lambheartedlion.org

ISBN: 978-0-9977758-3-9 - *hardcover*
ISBN: 978-0-9977758-4-6 - *softcover*
ISBN: 978-0-9977758-5-3 - *e-book*

*Illustrations*
John Harrison

*Book Design*
timmyroland.com

# UNCIRCUMCISED
WELCOMING LGBTQ PEOPLE INTO THE FAMILY OF GOD

# UNCIRCUMCISED
WELCOMING LGBTQ PEOPLE INTO THE FAMILY OF GOD

# ACKNOWLEDGMENTS

*My virtual friend, John Harrison* . . . Clearly, I am traveling a road less traveled. At times, I feel I walk alone on this path toward full inclusion and affirmation of my gender and sexual outlier friends and family. John is one of the rare few who travel this road with me. His artwork is thought provoking and challenging. I am entirely grateful for his chapter illustrations for this book and truly value his friendship on this lonely road. Please check out his work on guitargirlonline.net.

*My friends, Kelli, Tonya, Brian, Tom, Jennifer, Holly, Kelly, and everyone at the Uncomfortable Church* . . . I consider myself a "done"—someone once very religiously active but now done with all things church. Yet, I am drawn to various small group communities. The most helpful in my recovery from toxic church life has been the Uncomfortable Church. Our new friendships are challenging, inspiring, and ironically comforting!

*My unofficial debate partners who have engaged in mostly civil discourse in the so-called gay debates* . . . John, Pastor Wayne, Benjamin, and Stephanie—you have collectively represented the best of the non-affirming conscience to me. I hope you will continue this journey as we learn together.

*Jennifer Goossen and Travis Figg, two aspiring philosophers who gave critical feedback to this book* . . . Thank you for your insight and questions. You have helped improve my thoughts!

# UNCIRCUMCISED
WELCOMING LGBTQ PEOPLE INTO THE FAMILY OF GOD

# CONTENTS

**Acknowledgements** . . . . . . . . . . . . . . . . . . . . . . . . . . . . . *i*
**Introduction** . . . . . . . . . . . . . . . . . . . . . . . . . . . . . . . . . *v*
**Sin . . . and Consequences** . . . . . . . . . . . . . . . . . . . . . . 1
   The Sin of Sodom . . . . . . . . . . . . . . . . . . . . . . . . . . . 6
   The Lists . . . . . . . . . . . . . . . . . . . . . . . . . . . . . . . . . . 8
   The Exchanges . . . . . . . . . . . . . . . . . . . . . . . . . . . . . 16
   The Circumcision Party . . . . . . . . . . . . . . . . . . . . . 20
   No Hostility . . . . . . . . . . . . . . . . . . . . . . . . . . . . . . . 22
**Male and Female . . . and Eunuchs** . . . . . . . . . . . . 25
   The Garden of Eden . . . . . . . . . . . . . . . . . . . . . . . . 27
   Male and Female in the Law . . . . . . . . . . . . . . . . 29
   Three Kinds of Eunuchs . . . . . . . . . . . . . . . . . . . . 31
   No Male and Female . . . . . . . . . . . . . . . . . . . . . . . 34
**Marriage . . . and Suitability** . . . . . . . . . . . . . . . . . . 37
   The Purpose of Marriage . . . . . . . . . . . . . . . . . . . 40
   The Choice of Celibacy . . . . . . . . . . . . . . . . . . . . . 43
   The Bride Narrative . . . . . . . . . . . . . . . . . . . . . . . 45
   No Marriage . . . . . . . . . . . . . . . . . . . . . . . . . . . . . . 47
**Holiness . . . and Law** . . . . . . . . . . . . . . . . . . . . . . . . 51
   Respecting Conscience . . . . . . . . . . . . . . . . . . . . . 53
   Promoting Purity . . . . . . . . . . . . . . . . . . . . . . . . . . 56
   No Law . . . . . . . . . . . . . . . . . . . . . . . . . . . . . . . . . . 59
**Truth . . . and Questions** . . . . . . . . . . . . . . . . . . . . . 63
   Bible . . . . . . . . . . . . . . . . . . . . . . . . . . . . . . . . . . . . . 66
   Reason . . . . . . . . . . . . . . . . . . . . . . . . . . . . . . . . . . . 68
   Tradition . . . . . . . . . . . . . . . . . . . . . . . . . . . . . . . . . 74
   Spirit . . . . . . . . . . . . . . . . . . . . . . . . . . . . . . . . . . . . . 75
   Experience . . . . . . . . . . . . . . . . . . . . . . . . . . . . . . . 76
   No Fear . . . . . . . . . . . . . . . . . . . . . . . . . . . . . . . . . . 78

# UNCIRCUMCISED
WELCOMING LGBTQ PEOPLE INTO THE FAMILY OF GOD

# INTRODUCTION

> *"The church is faced with gay and lesbian Christians who exhibit many gifts and fruits of the Spirit and who seek to live in deep obedience to Christ. Many of these gay and lesbian Christians seek, not to suppress their sexual orientation, but rather to sanctify it, thus drawing intimate gay and lesbian relationships into the sanctifying work of the Spirit."*
> James V. Brownson, Bible, Gender, Sexuality: Reframing the Church's Debate on Same-Sex Relationships

There are LGBTQ people who are following Jesus. They display marks of the Holy Spirit. Their lifestyle shows evidence of a sanctified spirit, revealing all the qualities we Christians seek—goodness, kindness, holiness, and faithfulness.

Such a reality puts orthodox Christians and Biblical theologians in a difficult position. How are gender and sexual outliers to be included in God's plan and how are they to follow Jesus? Does God demand they conform to the male and female gender structures found in the Bible, and does this mean mandatory celibacy? Do we wait on decades of scientific research in order to welcome such people? I venture to guess the early Christians asked similar questions about uncircumcised Gentiles. How can someone who is uncircumcised be part of God's plan and follow Jesus? Don't they know God is a holy God? Does God's truth require believers to be circumcised according to the requirements for God's people?

You are right to care deeply about theology, the holy life of Jesus, and the liberating truth he taught. I care deeply about these as well. As Christians, we are charged with the task of finding what is hermeneutically revealed in the Bible if we are

# UNCIRCUMCISED

to welcome our LGBTQ friends and family. This is precisely what I begin to do in this book.

I concur with my non-affirming Christian friends on at least one point they repeatedly make: we cannot set aside the truth of God. Furthermore, we cannot ignore the fact that God is a holy God. I too care about such things. We who affirm same-sex relationships among our friends and family, and claim to be Christian, have answers we need to give. We have gone ahead with a love-first, figure-out-theology-later mentality—and I applaud that approach. However, I am suggesting now is the time to figure out that theology. Orthodoxy matters, along with orthopraxy and orthopathy. What we do and how we feel is just as significant, in my mind, as what we believe.

My primary contention is that in addition to the holy Life and the liberating Truth, Jesus is the effervescent Way. We focus on the truth, but what about the way and the life? The way of Jesus is often overlooked. Could anyone tell that Jesus hates sin by the way he interacted with people? Not really, no. At times, he seemed to indulge in sin! They called him a drunkard and a glutton, in fact.

Many in the American church have adopted a tension-filled stance toward homosexuality. Like myself not too long ago, they are caught somewhere in between blessing and condemnation. Such a conscience will neither permit full condemnation nor allow full blessing of people who fall outside the male and female constructs and the one-man, one-woman marriage arrangement. The best many can offer is a tearful shoulder to cry upon. What is remarkable to me is that such a stance reveals how weak the gospel has become in the American church. I am no longer surprised by the teachings about brokenness, sadness, and hopelessness presented to LGBTQ people. Such teachings are in fact what a flawed gospel produces.

Is the American church so out of touch with the gospel Jesus preached that we could only offer a tension-laced message of conformance based on conservative values, or an anything-goes, freestyle morality based on liberal values? While I can appreciate the conservative desire to remain faithful to the Bible and the liberal desire to give people freedom, I contend that this tension, in the end, is not healthy for the church or for society. Might not liberals actually care about the truth of God than they are given credit for? And maybe the conservatives really do care about freedom. In between these extremes sit the moderates, hoping everyone just calms down. It would seem impossible to bridge the gaps in the church exposed by the earthquake nature of the so-called gay debates.

In the end, I believe the tension arising from these debates is an example of bad fruit stemming from a gospel that is deceptively out of sync with the Bible. I make these claims because this tension typically turns into hostility or at best forms an uneasy truce among family members, causing pain, heartache, and misery. Such hostility is not of the Spirit. If the gaps between us are too large and no bridge can be made, then we all must begin walking toward each other.

My hope for this book not to build bridges, but to illuminate a path through the hostility and a way past the tension, for anyone—conservative, liberal or moderate—who should choose to walk such a path toward each other. While I do speak from a more liberal voice, I aim to demonstrate the good fruit of love, joy, peace, forbearance, kindness, goodness, faithfulness, gentleness, and self-control. Regardless of our viewpoint and regardless of what medical science reveals about the changing nature of gender identity and sexual orientation, my main point is this: should not the Christian church remove the hostility?

One of the many causes of the hostility over these sexuality issues, in my observation, is the lack of respect for each other, and specifically for those who do not accept same-sex marriage or who do not welcome those who are labeled as LGBTQ. The conscience of such people is often seen only in a negative light, and only known as non-affirming. There are many in the Christian church who do not affirm same-sex marriage as being good and who do not affirm the idea that human sexuality is a plurality of genders. Rather than reject such a conscience, I seek to respect the non-affirming conscience—specifically that conscience which welcomes, but does not affirm, our friends and family who do not fit into the binary ideas of "male and female".

Those who are stuck between condemnation and blessing are stuck, I believe, for valid reasons. Are we sinning by welcoming gender and sexual outliers into the church? Are we straying from God's natural design for gender by celebrating a new gender spectrum? Are we poisoning the sanctity of marriage by affirming same-sex marriage beyond "one man, one woman"? How can we include LGBTQ friends and family in the church and claim to know the holiness of a holy God? Are we setting aside the truth of God by joyfully celebrating with gender and sexual outliers? These are serious questions—each so blessedly simple to answer and yet each worthy of lengthy discourse. These five questions provide the structure for this book. Each chapter addresses one of these theological topics and how I see them applied in the LGBTQ arena: sin, gender, marriage, holiness, and truth.

I want to take you on a journey through these debates, as I encounter them, in order to illuminate new ways for the American Christian church to revisit the Bible, remove hostility, and affirm all people for who they are on their journey. Can the church do this in our lifetime? I say yes, the church can and must. Not only can the church remove the hostility, I see that the church has already navigated difficult, hostile issues in the past. The best example I find of the Christian church navigating a challenging issue is the debate that raged like wildfire in the first century church—the circumcision debate.

At first glance, there may seem to be no link between an ancient religious ceremony for males and the complex array of human sexuality that we reduce to an acronym of LGBTQ. Indeed, the topics are apples and oranges. However, consider this: what if you are adverse to fruit? In such a case, it matters not if we discuss apples, oranges, or bananas. If a person says fruit is bad in general, then the way to find a common link for discussion is by addressing why fruit is bad and perhaps look into why fruit could in fact be good.

This is the case with uncircumcised people and LGBTQ people. The situations are different, but both groups have been excluded from Christian fellowship. Both groups must deal with troublesome commands in the Bible. And both groups must deal with centuries of church tradition that opposes them.

How then, are the topics of circumcision and human sexuality related? The somewhat comical link is of course the religious obsession with male body parts, which never seems to go away. On a more serious note, the connections between how Christians approach uncircumcision and homosexuality are both numerous and illuminating. Both topics involve Old Covenant commands that are not positive, to say the least. To be uncircumcised meant to be intentionally excluded from God's people. The penalty for practicing homosexuality could mean death. Both topics have centuries of religious tradition supporting the supposed correct way of living—the Christian tradition appears to demand both circumcision and conformance to a male-and-female-only kind of society.

The idea that plagues Christians in many centuries is the idea that they must be against everything the Biblical laws are against. The notion often taught, even in modern American churches, is that Christians hate what God hates, and love what God loves, and the way we know what God hates is by studying the teachings in the Bible. Such a generalization is false, I claim, because the often Bible teaches contradictory principles. For example, the Bible teaches two opposing mandates about circumcision. One mandate is that circumcision is a requirement for belonging to the fellowship of God's people (i.e. Genesis 17:12; Exodus 12:48; Leviticus 12:3). The other mandate is that circumcision means nothing and is not a requirement for belonging to the fellowship of God's people (i.e. Acts 10:45; Galatians 6:15; Colossians 2:11-12). Such contradictory teachings may cause some to reject the Bible completely. Indeed, some people divorce themselves from the

# UNCIRCUMCISED

Bible and Christian theology, citing irreconcilable differences.

I do not reject the Bible however. The contradictory teachings, for me, are not a reason to reject the Bible, but an amazing opportunity to learn more from the Bible. The contradiction between circumcision and uncircumcision does not need to be an obstacle. Contradiction can be a profound teacher. I see much to learn from how the first century Christians found a way through the hostility formed by the circumcision debates. Those Christians were not only able to welcome but also to affirm their uncircumcised friends and family as truly part of their fellowship. Such a breakthrough did not open the proverbial Pandora's box, and required painful yet liberating discussion.

At first, the Christian leaders, such as Peter, could only welcome the uncircumcised with an uneasy tension. In Peter's mind, the uncircumcised could be present in their Christian fellowship, but they were not people with whom Peter would associate. Peter could welcome the uncircumcised, such as Titus, but did not consider such people as equal partners in his life and mission. Peter could not affirm something God calls unclean as being clean. When the times of eating together came, Peter did not sit in fellowship with the uncircumcised, but instead sat at the circumcised table. Such a welcome without affirmation was an offense to God, which Paul rightly pointed out to Peter through public rebuke. (Galatians 3; Acts 11)

Throughout this book, I attempt to employ the principles used by the first century Christian church, who found a way to both welcome and affirm people who are uncircumcised. I seek to pave the way for generations of Christians to welcome and affirm people who are not strictly male-and-female, but who are instead same-sex attracted, gender conflicted, sexually oppressed, or just plain confused and searching.

I invite you to walk with me through the so-called gay debates that permeate our generation. Because of these debates, I have delved more deeply into my Christian faith and looked more carefully at the Bible. I have adopted a love-first, figure-out-theology-later mentality, not only toward my LGBTQ friends and family, but also toward all people. I invite you to pause and listen to the ways I am working out this love-driven, gospel-affirming theology, centered on five topics: sin, gender, marriage, holiness, and truth. I present these topics, not as a systematic treatise or scientific research, but as a philosophical musing.

I believe it is time for the American church to study more deeply, to welcome more openly, and to affirm more clearly. It is also time for the American church to revisit, to apologize, and to listen—to the entire LGBTQ community and to other Christians. It is time to make amends for our un-Christ-like behavior. It is time to bring down the wall of hostility.

*"But no uncircumcised person shall eat of it."*
*Exodus 12:48*

# UNCIRCUMCISED
WELCOMING LGBTQ PEOPLE INTO THE FAMILY OF GOD

Brian John **Karcher**

*Yacoub & Tomás*
WORLDWIDE

UNCIRCUMCISED

# SIN... AND CONSEQUENCES

*"But the Scripture imprisoned everything under sin, so that the promise by faith in Jesus Christ might be given to those who believe."*
*Galatians 3:22 ESV*

The consequences of sin are bad. The consequences of sin-centric theology are worse. Hostility reigns where removing sin is preached as the gospel. America is now reaping this hostility before our very eyes—the fruit of decades of sincere American Christians who have tried to repent their way into Heaven by embarking on the impossible task of eradicating sin from their lives and from the world. Such a mission is just as futile as Sisyphus pushing his rock up the hill over and over again. Christians in America have been at the forefront of making sure we all know God hates sin and is not pleased with our performance. We hear stinging phrases hurled at us, such as "Go and sin no more!" and "You have not yet resisted sin to the point of shedding blood!" Such Biblical phrases are in fact correct, but were not spoken to everyone in every situation. Jesus only told one woman to "Go and leave your life of sin." (John 8:11) He did not give this direction to other people. In fact, Jesus did not even mention the word "sin" when talking with another woman (John 4).

On top of Bible verses taken out of context, we who welcome and affirm our LGTBQ friends and family often hear bad theology preached at us, such as "You have to love the sin, hate the sinner!" and "God says the gay lifestyle is sinful!".

# UNCIRCUMCISED

My non-Christian friends readily point out this hypocrisy, and rightly so. To "sin" has morphed into meaning "to go against what the church says about the Bible." Raising questions and expressing critical thinking have become futile tasks at best, and taboo actions at worst. Many of my friends relate to the following spirit from church leaders: "You are free to sit in our pews, give us money, and sometimes ask questions, but you must accept our answers or leave." Such a spirit can be found in both conservative-leaning and liberal-leaning churches.

The amazing new wine gospel has been lost. Christians are more commonly known as being against either LGBTQ people or other Christians, more than being known for loving one another. We have become old wineskins. The miraculous wine brought forth from water by our Lord has been spilling onto the dry ground, seeping back into the earth as we tightly cling to the dried up pieces of what is left of our wineskin. Hostility now permeates American society like yeast rising through dough.

Hostility, however, is neither new to the Christian church nor unique to Christians in America. The first century Christian church faced such hostility from the circumcision debates. Those in favor of circumcision had thousands of years of tradition and the full weight of clear commands from God on their side. Yet Paul the Apostle claimed circumcision was not necessary to be a believer in Christ. Paul was claiming that you could be fully accepted by God and even be a leader in the church—and be uncircumcised. Moreover, Paul went even further. Paul claimed to uphold the truth and holiness of God and was unashamedly against abuse of all kinds, and yet he fully affirmed the uncircumcised people. This boggled the minds of some early Christians, including Peter and John. I suspect that such a teaching invoked more havoc in those early days of Christianity than any of us have experienced in the so-called gay debates.

We have a handful of verses with debatable content; they had clear commands of God, such as in Genesis 17:11 . . . *you shall be circumcised!* Yet, the first century church survived the circumcision debate and removed the hostility by welcoming the uncircumcised. Were they contradicting God's truth? Were they disobeying a holy God?

Imagine the heated debates and rebukes the first church endured between the circumcised party and the uncircumcised party. Yes, that is correct—the Bible mentions that the opposition to being uncircumcised was so strong that they were a "party". Those who were in favor of being circumcised in the church were organized. They claimed God as their authority. Imagine the strong, Biblical case the circumcision proponents had on their side. Imagine how such people felt about Paul going around claiming he "saw the light of Jesus" and that believers did not have to be circumcised! What blasphemy, some thought. Paul was claiming the uncircumcised Gentiles were just as much Christians as the circumcised Jews. Many Christians wondered why a true believer in the God of Abraham would disobey the command of God so blatantly.

Somewhere along the line, the American church has become obsessed with sin. Perhaps this obsession is because we industrialize our forefather's Christianity, turning disciple making into an assembly line and the gospel into a formula for success. Perhaps our obsession with sin is rooted in the politicization of the church. Whatever the reason, the greatest correction needed in the American church today, in my mind, is a correction to our concept of sin. Surely, sin is a critical topic presented in the Bible. I am not saying we ignore sin. I am saying, on the contrary, that we find a way out of our obsession with sin and into a more healthy view of sin. The American church is so infatuated with identifying sin and removing sin, that we create what I call hyper-sins.

In contrast to sin, which is a wrong behavior or wrong attitude, a hyper-sin is a collection of many behaviors or attitudes considered wrong merely by association. I am hard-pressed to find any example of hyper-sins in the Biblical text. I find them only in church sermons or theological statements. For example, one hyper-sin invented by the church is the idea that being a Muslim is sinful. Now, it may in fact be true that some Muslims commit sins, but to collect all behaviors and attitudes of Muslims together and treat "being Muslim" as a sin is to create a hyper-sin. The reality is that many Muslims are in fact Godly and righteous people and are not being sinful just by being Muslim.

Homosexuality is one of these imagined hyper-sins. We have lumped homosexuality in with immorality, promiscuity, licentiousness, molestation, and all things pornographic in nature. Because our church communities have often associated homosexuality with sexual deviancy, our obsession with sin has gotten the best of us. Unraveling homosexuality from the abuse of sexuality, and untangling this sexual hyper-sin, goes a long way in removing the roadblocks that keep us from affirming LGBTQ friends and family. It is indeed the abuse of sex that the Bible condemns. Never is faithful love condemned as sinful.

Sin-centric theology hinders us from living out a foundational truth that marks most of the writings in the Bible. This truth is expressed in one of the first lessons of Galatians: *everything* is under sin. We *all* fall short. We are *all* sinners. No one is righteous. No one can obey the law of God well enough to earn God's favor. Not a single person will repent enough to remove sin completely from their life. The gospel message is not that we get super powers from Jesus to obey God and stop sinning, but that a way to God is opened up in spite of our sin, through the cross and the obedience of Jesus Himself. The promise of God comes by faith, not by removing sin.

This should not be so shocking, but I fear many will be ruffled by this statement: Not a single person will repent their way out of sin and into Heaven. Our repentance will never exceed our sin. The scales of justice are not in our favor. We will be found wanting. As soon as we point out the sin of our enemy, we judge ourselves. As soon as we express disgust for our neighbor's sin, we expose our own sin. The attempts, then, in Christian preaching, to single out someone else's sin, are futile. The more we point out other people's sins, the more we dig our own grave. The word of God in Galatians calls us to shed our sin-centric thinking and become faith-centric: "But the Scriptures imprisoned everything under sin, so that the promise by faith in Jesus Christ might be given to those who believe." (Galatians 3:22). We must live by faith because we cannot remove sin completely.

A wonderful story contrasting sin-centric thinking with faith-centric thinking is found in Luke 7:36-50. This is the story of Simon the Pharisee, who invited Jesus to dinner one day. Simon the Pharisee embodies the "love the sinner, hate the sin" theology so common today. The attitude behind this theology is more correctly stated as "tolerate the sinner, punish the sin". This attitude keeps Simon the Pharisee separated from "sinners" so much that he does not acknowledge a woman in his house, sitting at Jesus' feet. When Simon finally does see this woman, he thinks, "she is a sinner" and "why is she here"? In contrast, Jesus rebukes Simon with a lesson on forgiveness and says, "She loved much". In Simon's mind, this woman is a sinner acting inappropriately. He sees her as a sinner whose presence may be tolerated but whose person does not belong in his house. In Jesus' mind, this woman is a person who loved much. She is a person who not only deserves to be acknowledged, but honored for her actions toward Jesus. She belongs in the house. If there is anything my LGBTQ friends and family want, it is to belong as people.

What goes through our minds when we see LGBTQ people? What do we think when we see them in our churches? When we keep thinking "but they are sinners", we create a wall of hostility between people. When sin and the removal of sin is at the forefront of our lives, we become blind to those who love Jesus, even though they are right in front of us. We may even come to doubt our own love for Jesus. In time, such sin-centered thinking becomes self-destructive, as we discover that we cannot cut out sin fast enough from our own lives. Hostility reigns in the house where sin-centric theology is preached. How then do we remove such hostility? How do we move from "but they are sinners" to "but they love much"?

# UNCIRCUMCISED

## THE SIN OF SODOM

Concerning homosexuality, we have heard that the story of Sodom and Gomorrah in the Bible depicts God's wrath against homosexual sin, and that the story condemns them as sinners if they remain as such. I am stunned that so many have accepted this teaching without going deeper into the story itself. The teaching of God's judgment on the two cities being caused by homosexuality stems from a superficial reading of the text and a pathetic interpretation of the story. The story of Genesis 19 is irrelevant to the debates regarding LGBTQ people and their role in the church because the Genesis 19 stories speak to the sins of gang rape, abandonment, and inhospitality—all abominations to the Lord—and says nothing about faithful, loving relationships.

Yet, those who would push us toward a condemning attitude continue to bring up the story. I tire of writing about this, but I will continue to do so. Actually, I will let Tom Otto tell the story. His excellent book, *Oriented to Faith: Transforming the Conflict over Gay Relationships*, is very much worth the read. Tom has this to say about Genesis 19:

> *"When God sends angels to Sodom to see whether the city is as bad as the "outcry that has come to me" (Gen 18:21), Lot makes them "a feast" (19:3)—hospitality that ancient Near Eastern cultures would have venerated. In contrast to that hospitality, "the men of Sodom, both young and old, all the people to the last man," surround the house and demand to have sex with the visitors. From a Biblicist perspective, "the sin of Sodom" is perceived as homosexuality. The Sunday school flannel-graph boards of my childhood conveyed the horror of people being turned into sulfur, and I grew up thinking that this was clear evidence of God's disgust with homosexuals. I pondered the story of Sodom and Gomorrah and wondered, "Does God find me disgusting?" But a deeper reading of this story reveals that the men of Sodom were not threatening the angels with the "sin" of homosexuality, but rather with gang rape. In the ancient world, raping another*

man—thus putting him in the "woman's role"—was an act of cruel humiliation. Sodom was not an ancient gay spa, but a town with married men, women, and their children." (location 1745, Kindle edition)

From the text of Genesis 19, we can certainly see the sin of gang rape. But is there something more profound to learn here? For some unexplainable reason, I still believe in the authority of the Bible. Yes, I really do believe the Bible has the final say in my faith. As such, I give much credence to what the Bible has to say about the sin of Sodom. I read several statements about Sodom's sin in the book of Ezekiel that, to me, require little explanation. None of what the Bible says about the sin of Sodom has anything to do with our LGBTQ friends and family, unless of course they want to engage in gang rape.

We do not have to guess Sodom's sin. Ezekiel tells us. "Behold, this was the guilt of your sister Sodom: she and her daughters had pride, excess of food, and prosperous ease, but did not aid the poor and needy. They were haughty and did an abomination before me. So I removed them, when I saw it." (Ezekiel 16:49-50). The intention to commit gang rape is indeed an abomination, not merely for the nature of the crime, but because it was an act of supreme inhospitality. Not caring for the needy is a most tragic sin in the eyes of God. Inhospitality is an abomination to God.

This story in Genesis points out another abomination that is often overshadowed by the other conversations. Why do we tend to overlook the fact that in the story, Lot also offered his two daughters to the men outside his house? This is an atrocity. If the church is to have any credibility, we must call out the abomination of men standing by idly while young women are subjected to sexual crimes.

So then, we can begin to make right judgments about the situation of parents who have children who are transgender or lesbian or queer or bi-sexual. We can start to rightly judge those who commit sexual crimes such as rape. How are you treating your LGBTQ children? Do you stand by idly when you discover sexual abuse? Perhaps you may dismiss sexual abuse because you think to yourself "At least they are not gay…" Kicking children out of your house because you think they are Sodomites is a most self-condemning act. Treating abuse survivors with inhospitality or limiting the rights of LGBTQ people is in no way standing for the truth of God—it is tempting the wrath of God. It is not sexual unorthodoxy that gets God's knickers in a twist; it is failing to care for other people.

Genesis 19 is a bittersweet story that brings us face to face with the ugly side of humanity. The story reflects the worst of us. Perhaps the benefit of this story lies in the correction of our concept of sin. To be inhospitable is to sin. To mistreat our daughters, sons, friends, neighbors, or family members is an affront to God with dire consequences. To abuse sex, making sex into a weapon of humiliation and rape—that is what angers God. To abandon your daughter is sin. To cast out your son is sin. To refuse care for the needy among us is a sin. These sins are what invoke the wrath of God.

## THE LISTS

After realizing the story of Sodom and Gomorrah is not relevant to the LGBTQ topics such as same-sex marriage, the dreaded "lists of sins" normally come into play. The gay debates rage onward. Typically, those who argue that we must challenge the so-called gay lifestyle as sinful, will bring up the lists of sins found in the Bible as proof-positive that God rejects homosexuality entirely as sin. There is however, much room for debate.

The list of sins that repeatedly arises in the LGBTQ discussions is found in the Bible in these verses: 1st Corinthians 6:9-10 "Or do you not know that the unrighteous will not inherit the kingdom of God? Do not be deceived: neither the sexually immoral, nor idolaters, nor adulterers, nor men who practice homosexuality, nor thieves, nor the greedy, nor drunkards, nor revilers, nor swindlers will inherit the kingdom of God."

Until the 1940's, the historical, traditional interpretation of these verses, written by Paul the Apostle, describe the abuse of something—the abuse of sex, the abuse of religion, the abuse of marriage, the abuse of male bodies, the abuse of property rights of others, the abuse of alcohol, and the abuse of money. Paul goes on in the verses right after this to say that some of the Christians were just that—thieves, murderers, abusers—and he calls on them to stop abusing such things for they have been washed in Jesus.

Why then is this list brought up to exclude our LGBTQ friends and family? Reasons for this rather recent theological stance can be found by observing history. Kathy Baldock has the most profound exposition of this history, in her book *Walking the Bridgeless Canyon*. Here I want to highlight two striking events that Kathy speaks about in depth. I believe these two events are most at fault for the church going beyond the teaching of avoiding abuse. If you have not encountered Kathy's work, I suggest you put down this book and go listen to her speak. *(To learn more about Kathy's work, search for "Kathy Baldock: Untangling the Mess - The Reformation Project in Los Angeles" on youtube.com)*

One event Kathy explains well is the morphing of the Bible translations over the years. Why has the church jumped into the gay debates so strongly in recent decades? One answer is the recent addition of the word "homosexual" to the Bible. As Kathy wonderfully describes, the word "homosexuality" does not belong in 1st Corinthians 6:9-10. Why translate this ancient verse about abuse into English using a word that was coined in the late 1800's and has nothing to do with abuse of any kind? The word does not fit the context in any sense.

The Greek words used in the verses above are anything but clear. Thus, Bible translators have had a difficult time finding the correct English terms to represent the words "malakos" and "arsenokoitai" found in 1 Corinthians 6:9-10. The attempt to translate these words into English began in the 1600's with

## UNCIRCUMCISED

the King James Bible. The translation in the King James Bible is "abusers of themselves with mankind". While I am not a King-James-only type of person, I find this translation to be sufficient in this case. Should not a list of abuses contain words related to abuse?

In 1946, the word homosexuality was first popularized by a commentary published alongside an English Bible translation. The Revised Standard Version (RSV) renders 1st Corinthians 6:9-10 this way: "Do you not know that the unrighteous will not inherit the kingdom of God? Do not be deceived; neither the immoral, nor idolaters, nor adulterers, nor sexual perverts, nor thieves, nor the greedy, nor drunkards, nor revilers, nor robbers will inherit the kingdom of God." Notice the words correctly used are "sexual perverts" and not "homosexuals", as in later translations. Commentary on this RSV translation, however, inserted the word "homosexuals" into the thought fabric of Bible readers.

As Kathy explains, the commentary on the 1946 RSV Bible by George A. Buttrick combines two Greek terms, "malakos" and "arsenokoitai", into one term, "homosexual". This approach caught on quickly. Dozens of Bible translation efforts followed Buttrick's commentary until the word "homosexuals" was added into the Bible text itself. Thus, the recent church anger against gender and sexual outliers could be said to have begun in the 1940's. To be homosexual became equivalent to being sexually perverted.

Further complicating the Bible translation confusion is a popular America preacher named Kenneth Taylor. Again, I point to Kathy's work where she describes Taylor's ideas about creating a paraphrase for children to understand. Starting around 1971, Taylor's paraphrase, The Living Bible, was popularized by the Billy Graham crusades. Listen to the words used by Taylor's paraphrasing of 1st Corinthians 6:9-10: "Don't you know that those doing such things have no share in the Kingdom of God? Don't fool yourselves. Those who live immoral lives, who are idol worshipers, adulterers or homosexuals—will have no share in his Kingdom. Neither will thieves or greedy people, drunkards, slanderers, or robbers."

It is estimated that over 40 million copies of The Living Bible paraphrase were given away at Billy Graham's rallies. Thus, the nuance of the two Greek terms used in a few verses of the Bible to describe specific abusive sexual behavior is lost in translation. The idea that homosexuals have no place in God's kingdom became embedded into the Fundamentalist and Evangelical psyche. The paraphrased English word "homosexual", a much broader term that describes orientation and attractiveness, replaced the two specific terms Apostle Paul used in the original Greek text.

At the time, in the 1960's and 1970's, this translation seemed natural to some people, since the prevailing thought was that homosexuality was a mental disorder that could be cured. The medical science journals of the time labeled homosexuality as a disorder—an abuse of the body caused by mental problems. Therefore, the Bible translators thought they had found a better word for the Greek text.

I find this fact about the rather recent addition of the phrase "men who practice homosexuality" into the English Bible to be helpful in answering questions about the church's reactions to our LGBTQ friends and family. Homosexuals have certainly existed for eons, but why the rather sudden fixation by the English-speaking churches? Could it be that the word "homosexual" does not accurately capture what Bible authors meant to say? Indeed, this loss of nuance in a couple verses has been a primary catalyst for the recent entrenchment of churches, especially in America, against homosexuality.

The second significant event I want to point out from Kathy's book occurred in 1973. That is when the American Psychological Association removed the term homosexuality from its list of mental disorders. Later, in 1990, the World Health Organization de-classified homosexuality as well, thereby declaring that homosexuality is neither a disease that needs curing nor a disorder that needs repairing. While the Christian world struggled to understand her new Bible translations, the secular world wrestled with medical science. The world discovered that homosexuality has nothing to do with abuse or disorder or any other significant flaw in the human body. The church however, was sent into a downward spiral of division and heartache throughout the 1980's and 1990's. Churches are still reeling from the impact today.

In the end, however, we are left with a stunning fact: the Bible translators have difficulty translating the Greek into English. So if, over the course of over 70 years, the Bible linguistic experts cannot agree on what words to use to describe the sins on the list in Corinthians, what are we to do? For starters, I say the translators ought to make one more attempt, and use words that describe abuse of some kind. In context, the abuse of sex is what makes sense in 1st Corinthians 6:9-10. Christians ought to be against the abuses on Paul's lists, for it is the abuse of sex that must be challenged and corrected, not the complex nature of human sexuality. No matter how we translate the Greek words here, all of them point to abuse of some kind. Abusing ourselves or other people is indeed a sin to be avoided.

Until the Bible translators decide to account for these ideas, we are left with Bibles translated using the word homosexuality on the list of sins to avoid. And so the list stings. This list supposes there is no hope for our LGBTQ friends unless they conform to the typical two-gender, male-and-female society (i.e. girls wear pink clothes, boys where blue clothes; marriage can only be one man, one woman…) Such conformance has proved massively difficult, and in reality impossible, for generation after generation of LGBTQ people. Thus, the hope offered by many Christians becomes one of extreme duress and harmful tension. Many are caught between fully condemning and fully blessing our gender minority friends and family. The all-surpassing gospel hope presented in the Bible remains elusive when we instruct gender outliers to shoehorn themselves into our American male-and-female moral constructs and social norms.

There is hope however, even with the current translations of the Bible. My thought is that intricate linguistic gymnastics are not needed in order to derive meaning from the list of sins. For example, what about the other lists of grave sins? Those lists make no mention of homosexuality in any way. Jesus has his own list of grave sins. "For out of the heart come evil thoughts, murder, adultery, sexual immorality, theft, false witness, slander. These are what defile a person. But to eat with unwashed hands does not defile anyone." (Matthew 15:19-20) Nothing here in Jesus' list explicitly describes homosexual activity or bans faithful, loving LGBTQ relationships.

John gives us another list in Revelations 21:8 "But as for the cowardly, the faithless, the detestable, as for murderers, the sexually immoral, sorcerers, idolaters, and all liars, their portion will be in the lake that burns with fire and sulfur, which is the second death." Again, this list makes no mention explicitly of homosexuals or gender outliers.

If men committing homosexual acts are so very displeasing to God, why is such activity not called out on every list of sins? I suggest that if we are seeking a comprehensive list of sins to avoid as part of our quest for holiness, we have missed the mark entirely. If we are obsessed with the question, "What is sin?" it seems we will have little time for the question Jesus emphasized, "What is love?"

How then do we navigate all these lists of sins we find in the Bible, especially since they differ significantly? First off, I propose that the intention of the lists is not to go around determining who is on what list. If we think the intention of the new covenant initiated on the cross is about conforming to moral lists, we would be better off going back to the old covenant. What sense does it make for Jesus, who fulfilled the 613 old covenant commands to demand us to conform to a list of over 1,000 new covenant commands? Surely, there is something more to the all-surpassing, effervescent, new wine gospel of joy!

The lists in the new covenant seem to me to be the result

# UNCIRCUMCISED

of the Biblical authors attempting to contextualize the grace and love they discovered from Jesus. They were trying to figure out how to influence the culture around them with the mercy-centric good news about Jesus. The early Christians wished to infuse society with love, truth, mercy, justice, and grace. Therefore, these lists of sins in the Bible are examples of freedom mixed with restraint. The Bible frees Christians from being bound to holiness codes and yet exhorts Christians to be against abuse and harmful practices, all within the constraints of the Holy Spirit and faithful love.

To highlight this point, I turn to the events described in Acts 15. Some Christians were demanding Gentile Christians to conform to a list of Old Covenant rules, such as: celebrate the Passover, abstain from pork, and most importantly, be circumcised. We see examples of this all over Paul's writings to the Corinthians, the Ephesians, and the other early churches. In time, the dietary rules faded and so did the observance of religious ceremonies prescribed in the Old Covenant. Nevertheless, circumcision remained a powerfully dividing issue.

At the time, those who supported circumcising Christian believers were loudly preaching their lists of moral conformance. They demanded obedience to God's commands, such as in Leviticus 12:3 "And on the eighth day the flesh of his foreskin shall be circumcised." There are no loopholes in this command from God—case closed. Be circumcised or you are not of God. Be circumcised or you are not allowed to be a leader in the Christian church. Be circumcised or you are not a true believer. They pointed to the stories of their tradition, which had been in place since Abraham, for over 2,000 years. They looked to the stories of God's people, such as Joshua: "At that time the Lord said to Joshua, 'Make flint knives and circumcise the sons of Israel a second time.'" (Joshua 5:2).

In spite of this overwhelming Scriptural clarity about circumcision, what did the early church do? They attempted to settle the matter of uncircumcised Gentiles with the first council, held in Jerusalem. We read about this in Acts 15. The circumcision supporters were teaching this: "Unless you are circumcised according to the custom of Moses, you cannot be saved." (Acts 15:1) Circumcision was so deeply embedded in the religious culture of the time that circumcision became a requirement for salvation! The supporters of circumcision were not swayed by the joyful work of the Spirit among the uncircumcised Gentiles. The circumcision party was relentless. After witnessing the work of the Spirit among the Gentile Christians, they held fast to their teaching: "It is necessary to circumcise them and to order them to keep the law of Moses." (Acts 15:5)

In response to those who demanded circumcision for salvation, the apostles and elders gathered. They prayed and debated. Finally, after much debate, Peter stood up and shared a most remarkable speech.

> "Brothers, you know that in the early days God made a choice among you, that by my mouth the Gentiles should hear the word of the gospel and believe. And God, who knows the heart, bore witness to them, by giving them the Holy Spirit just as he did to us, and he made no distinction between us and them, having cleansed their hearts by faith. Now, therefore, why are you putting God to the test by placing a yoke on the neck of the disciples that neither our fathers nor we have been able to bear? But we believe that we will be saved through the grace of the Lord Jesus, just as they will." (Acts 15:7-11)

This is breathtaking.

After Peter's remarks, the council sat in stunned silence. It was a moment of realization, a moment of calm just before the waves of incredible all-surpassing joy flooded their hearts! Then Paul and Barnabas broke the silence and recounted the signs and wonders God had done among the uncircumcised. The excitement in the room was palpable. What is this new thing God is doing among the uncircumcised?

# UNCIRCUMCISED

After hearing the faith of uncircumcised Gentile Christians, the Jewish Christians immediately recall the words of Amos the prophet. With new clarity, they revisit Amos 9:11-15, not with pride in their nation Israel, but with compassion for those outside Israel. That compassion for Gentiles is how their nation is restored. That compassion for the outsider, for "Edom", is what reveals the glory of God. Then they realize God had already envisioned the uncircumcised calling on the name of the Lord.

Is there such compassion for gender and sexual outliers? What verses in the Bible can we turn to and revisit in a new light? In regard to gender—male and female—there are several Bible verses to revisit. I will get to those verses in the other chapters in this book. The topic at hand however, is that of disobeying the direct command of God. What a concept! Can believers intentionally and directly disobey a command from God? If the command of God is to be circumcised, how can we disobey God and not be circumcised?

We read in Acts 15 that Peter, James and John decided to make a new list. They intentionally set aside God's commands to be circumcised, not out of sinful spite but out of obedience to the Holy Spirit. Their letter to the Gentile Christians was short and contained a list of only three directions. The uncircumcised were to avoid idolatry, avoid sexual immorality, and avoid eating meat or blood from strangled animals. In more common terms, the council's advice is this: Love God, do not abuse sex, and respect the religions of other people. Is it not possible for the 21st century Christian church to do the same? Is not this list exactly the advice we ought to give LGBTQ Christians?

## THE EXCHANGES

At this point in the debate about homosexuality, both sides are usually worn out. Those who insist on proving homosexuality is a sin will not be deterred by new insight into Genesis 19 or by the knowledge about the words used in the list in Corinthians.

With dogged determination unmatched except perhaps by the circumcision party, the homosexuality-is-sin party moves onto the great exchange in the first chapter of the book of Romans. This is proof-positive, they claim, that God is not pleased by the so-called gay lifestyle of LGBTQ Christians.

However, Romans chapter one is hardly a comprehensive sexual guidance manual. Instead, the chapter is the opening act in a grand opera of magnificent proportions. It saddens me to see how this chapter has been confiscated as some sort of proof-text condemnation of LGBTQ Christians when the text is a grand theological construct. I for one am not up to the challenge of fully explaining all the chapters in Romans. However, let us take a closer look at how the first chapter has typically been applied in the LGBTQ realm.

In Romans 1:18-31, we see not one, but three exchanges. All three are about people giving up on God. They exchange something of God for something of the world. The exchanges are described as the exchange of God's glory for idols, the exchange of God's truth for lies, and the exchange of natural sex for lust. At the end of these exchanges, we find yet another list, which in fact says nothing about homosexuality directly: "They were filled with all manner of unrighteousness, evil, covetousness, malice. They are full of envy, murder, strife, deceit, maliciousness. They are gossips, slanderers, haters of God, insolent, haughty, boastful, inventors of evil, disobedient to parents, foolish, faithless, heartless, ruthless." (Romans 1:29-31).

The claim that these exchanges have anything to say about faithful, loving same-sex relationships is ludicrous to me, at best. The author's point here has nothing to do with singling out certain people and condemning their lifestyle or their nature. In fact, the text makes it impossible to say the LGBTQ relations cause God's wrath. The valid point that can be made is that God's wrath is upon all human beings—homosexuals and heterosexuals alike. The exchanges in Romans 1 do not bring about God's wrath, but are in fact a result of God's wrath—not on one specific kind of people but on all people. The specific mention of homosexual and lesbian lust in this text does not preclude the existence of faithful, loving relationships among LGBTQ people. In short, Romans 1 tells us God is angry with everyone.

Turning the page to Romans chapter two makes this point explicitly: "Therefore you have no excuse, O man, every one of you who judges. For in passing judgment on another you condemn yourself, because you, the judge, practice the very same things?" (Romans 2:1-3)

The discussion usually ends at this point, at least in my experience. Both sides leave in silence and the hostility rolls in like a thick fog. The first chapter of Romans solves nothing in the gay debates.

Here is what one New Testament scholar, Jim Brownson, has to say about the exchanges in Romans chapter 1, in his book, *Bible, Gender, Sexuality: Reframing the Church's Debate on Same-Sex Relationships*, on page 150:

> *"Before exploring lust and desire more specifically, however, it is important to get an accurate picture of the overall flow of Paul's thought in this opening of his letter to the Romans. These verses are part of a larger section of Romans (1:18–3:20), and the overall goal of this larger section is to demonstrate the universal sinfulness of humanity and the universal need of humanity for the salvation that is found in Paul's gospel (1:16). Paul concludes this larger section beginning in Romans 3:9 by saying, "We have already charged that all, both Jews and Greeks, are under the power of sin." He follows with a long list of the Bible quotations affirming the universality of human sinfulness. Within this larger section, Romans 1:18-32 focuses on the sinfulness of Gentiles who are "without excuse" (1:20) in their sinfulness and their refusal to worship the true God, even though they have not received the law. Paul argues that the truth about God God's eternal power and deity is plain to them in the created order (1:20). The core Gentile problem is idolatry:*

> *it is their refusal to worship the true God and instead their devotion to "images resembling a mortal human being or birds or four-footed animals or reptiles" (1:23). This practice of idolatry constitutes rebellion against God, and as a result God hands them over "in the lusts of their hearts to impurity, to the degrading of their bodies among themselves" (1:24). The verses following verse 24 depict a cascading and intensifying montage of evil and corruption that culminates in a list of twenty-one separate vices in Romans 1:29-31."*

This letter to the Romans was never intended to be a treatise on sexual ethics. Nothing is written here in chapter 1, or any chapter, about faithful, loving, same-sex relationships. Therefore, instead of looking to Romans 1 to either prove or disprove the church's reaction to our LGBTQ friends and family, I suggest we look at a major teaching from these exchanges found in this chapter. What correction to sin is here?

I find a most amazing teaching here in Romans 1 in regard to sin: we have all exchanged something for sin, and it is only by faith that we can live a righteous life. Have we gotten so off track that we miss this profound gospel truth? Many have looked at Romans 1 only to miss verses 16 and 17: "For I am not ashamed of the gospel, for it is the power of God for salvation to everyone who believes, to the Jew first and also to the Greek. For in it the righteousness of God is revealed from faith for faith, as it is written, "The righteous shall live by faith."

All people—gay, straight, or otherwise—have fallen short of God's standard. The gospel truth presented in Romans 1 is that we cannot rid our world or ourselves of sin entirely, and that our one hope is faith in God's forgiveness. Getting rid of sin, then, is not what makes us clean. Faith is our hope.

Much more discussion is needed to understand something of the masterpiece that is Romans in the Bible. Such discussion is beyond the scope of this book and only goes on to further demonstrate the fact that all people are in need of the grace of God and the mercy of each other. No distinction is made anywhere in Romans regarding homosexual versus

# UNCIRCUMCISED

heterosexual. There is not one single gay exception clause to any of the magnificent gospel promises put forth in Paul's letter to the Romans. We have all exchanged something for sin, and we cannot undo that exchange. We move forward by faith.

## THE CIRCUMCISION PARTY

In the first century church, the opposition to welcoming and affirming uncircumcised Christians gained massive support. They became to be known as "the circumcision party". Even Peter was criticized by them. How dare Peter, the exemplary Christian, allow uncircumcised Christians into the church? (Acts 11:2-3) Perhaps it is this kind of criticism that persuaded Peter to not eat at the table of his fellow uncircumcised Christians. Friction certainly sparked between Peter and Titus, a leader in the church who was not circumcised. Titus struggled with the circumcision party repeatedly. The party was upsetting entire families by what Titus calls "empty talk" and for "shameful gain" (Titus 1:9-11). Titus calls those who advocate for the circumcision requirement as "insubordinate".

This is fascinating to me. Those who preached obedience to God's law requiring circumcision are called insubordinate by the early church leaders. Did you catch that? Those who were striving to obey God's law were being disobedient to the Holy Spirit. This reveals to me the general mindset of the early Christians. They regarded obedience to the Holy Spirit and to the gospel as far more important than obedience to specific laws and precepts of God. This is not to say they begrudged the laws of God. It is to say however, that they let the Spirit move them beyond external obedience to holiness codes and into a relationship with Jesus as Lord and with each other, no matter how different people were from each other. Jew and Gentile, Greek and Samaritan—they found a way out of hostility and chose to live in peace with each other. This did not happen, however, without much pain.

The hostility in the early church escalated until Paul the Apostle could not take it anymore. Paul was still persecuted even when he acknowledged the validity of circumcision! He was in a difficult situation. And so he expresses his frustration candidly: "But if I, brothers, still preach circumcision, why am I still being persecuted? In that case the offense of the cross has been removed. I wish those who unsettle you would emasculate themselves!" (Galatians 5:7-12)

Paul's words here are stunning. If the circumcision party wants circumcision, Paul says do not stop with cutting off the tip, cut the whole thing off! *Emasculate yourself!*

At this point in the gay debates, I often feel this way—exasperated. How can we move forward? While it may be convenient for some in the church to conclude the debate here and live with a "love the sinner, hate the sin" mindset, such an attitude does nothing to remove the hostility that hangs in the air. Such an attitude is most tragic to children and adults who have grown up with the Bible and church-going life. Some people may be able to move on without the Bible, surmising that for them at least, it is fine to set aside the Bible as merely an ancient text that no longer applies to our lives. In fact, if the church does not resolve the hostility and tension caused by not welcoming and affirming our LGBTQ friends and family, we may very well be better off moving on without the Bible.

For some Christians, these conclusions do not sit well. Many Christians are left with a hostile tension. We feel trapped by the Bible—not able to fully bless our LGBTQ brothers and sisters and not willing to fully celebrate them for who they are. The cloud of sorrow hangs over our heads each Sunday. The wonderful sermons about other topics seem dull and lifeless with each passing week. My contention is that the gay debates have lead the church into a wall of hostility because we have failed to see the gospel truths hidden in the closet. How do we remove the damaging hostility that lurks around every corner?

# UNCIRCUMCISED

## NO HOSTILITY

Is hostility one of the marks of the Christian church? Are Christians encouraged to be identified by our hostility anywhere in the Bible? The answer is a resounding no. Christians have no choice in this matter. Love demands us to remove hostility. Christians who live in continual hostility live outside the will of God. If we are content with living in the midst of hostility, I contend that we have much to learn about Christ. Hostility is not a mark of Christianity. Yet concerning LGBTQ issues, is not our present day American church brimming with hostility underneath all that holy paint?

The early church found the solution—the cross on which the Christ was crucified. Ponder their thoughts for a moment:

> *"For he himself is our peace, who has made us both one and has broken down in his flesh the dividing wall of hostility by abolishing the law of commandments expressed in ordinances, that he might create in himself one new man in place of the two, so making peace, and might reconcile us both to God in one body through the cross, thereby killing the hostility."* (Ephesians 2:14-16).

If Christ killed the hostility, why do we foster hostility? The circumcision party and the anti-circumcision party were reconciled by realizing one astounding truth: Christ set aside in his flesh the law. They did not live in holy tension long term. Through the circumcision debates, the early church came to the cross, learned a deeper truth, and rejoiced in a new reality. Peter, James and John extended the right hand of fellowship to those who affirmed uncircumcised believers—Paul, Barnabas and Titus.

Indeed, God did require circumcision as a sign of being a true believer in the past. Now however the covenant shifted. No longer is the sign of faith a cutting of man's flesh as prescribed by the circumcision ritual. The sign of faith is in Christ's flesh. No longer are the commands and regulations of the Old Covenant our supervisor for morality. No longer is the Law of the Old Covenant the guardian of the church. No more are we to conform to the Old Covenant sexual ethics or societal constructs (Galatians 3). In the New Covenant, the Holy Spirit is our guide and love is our plumb line.

I believe such good news is the effervescent new wine of Jesus. Upon learning this reality found in the cross—that the mark of faith is in Christ, not in us—my whole world shifted. I found the peace that passes all understanding. I found contentment in all circumstances. I discovered why the teachers of the law were angered to the point of crucifying Christ. Such truth removes hostility in me, not only toward LGBTQ people but also toward my enemies, my strangers, my neighbors, other Christians, and perhaps most importantly—toward myself.

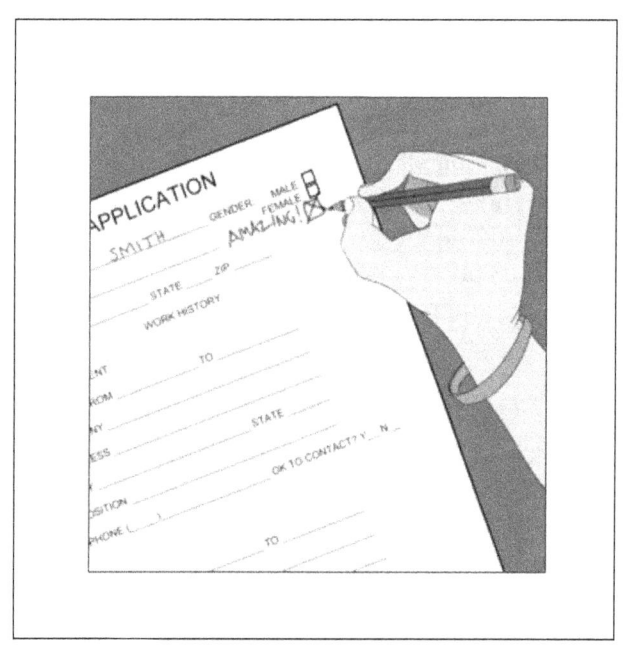

UNCIRCUMCISED

# MALE AND FEMALE... AND EUNUCHS

> *"There is neither Jew nor Greek, there is neither slave nor free, there is no male and female, for you are all one in Christ Jesus."*
>
> *- Galatians 3:28 ESV*

When I raise the topic of eunuchs in the Bible, nearly all of my friends cringe, whether affirming or non-affirming. My affirming friends are typically not so fond of any association of eunuchs with LGBTQ people, for they are different in many ways. While I agree that the Bible is not speaking about LGBTQ people directly in the eunuch stories, I contend that there are wonderful messages to be found in such stories that are relevant. For example, the first person approached in Acts after Stephen's death and the subsequent persecution is a eunuch—a person who is not fully male or female. Neither Philip nor the Holy Spirit is recorded as saying anything about the eunuch's sexual life or gender condition (Acts 8:26-40). Conforming into the gender binary (male and female biological gender and opposite-sex attraction) is not a requirement for faith in this story. In fact, no verse anywhere in the Bible adds such a gender conformance requirement—not for salvation, not for faith, not for acceptance, and not for receiving blessing.

Those who are non-affirming also cringe when I bring up the topic of eunuchs, but for different reasons. Some of them have not realized Jesus talked about three kinds of eunuchs in the very passage they quote to prove there are only male and female genders (Matthew 19). Others are just too grossed out by eunuchs, and no longer wish to discuss such matters. Still others dismiss the eunuch stories all together, claiming all eunuchs are males and therefore have nothing to contribute to the discussion.

In any case, those who do continue the discussion tend to move on from the topic of sin and raise the issue of gender. They present to me the "male and female" argument, typically quoting these words of Jesus: "Have you not read that he who created them from the beginning made them male and female, and said, 'Therefore a man shall leave his father and his mother and hold fast to his wife, and the two shall become one flesh'?" (Matthew 19:4-5) Case closed, they say. Jesus says there is only male and female, and that only opposite genders attract to each other in God's best design.

Such a superficial glance at the Bible rarely leads to a healthy conclusion. What does the Bible as a whole say about how "male and female" should behave? What do we find when we look at the entire context of Jesus' words in Matthew 19? Such questions compel me to re-read the Bible from a gender-aware viewpoint. What gender language is being used in the text? Are we mandated to implement such gender language in our current generation? Read this way, we immediately see the Bible is steeped in male-dominate language. While there are remarkable reformations in the language constructs found in the Bible, such as including women in genealogies, the Bible is written overwhelmingly with the idea of a male-dominate, gender binary, patronymic hierarchy.

Are we therefore constrained to the centuries old gendered language used in the Bible? Is a two-gender construct and a male-dominated gender hierarchy God's only creation? Why do some people deem gender plurality to be a great evil? Must we bind gender to the gospel? What I find is one of the most fascinating, amazing, and revealing threads in the entire Bible!

## THE GARDEN OF EDEN

The Biblical thread of "male and female" of course begins in Genesis. This is what Jesus refers to when he answers a question about divorce: "This is the book of the generations of Adam. When God created man, he made him in the likeness of God. Male and female he created them, and he blessed them and named them Man when they were created." (Genesis 5:1-2)

At this point in the debates, my non-affirming friends often resort to the childish argument that "God made Adam and Eve, not Adam and Steve!" This is not so much an argument as it is a reaction to realizing the Bible does not support an anti-LGBTQ position as clearly some once thought.

When I hear this "God's design" argument, my first reaction is to point out that we do not live in the Garden of Eden. The Bible narrative tells us we are living after the event called the Fall of Man, whereby the woman in the Garden, Eve, tempted Adam to eat the forbidden fruit from the one tree about which God said, "Do not eat the fruit." Nothing is the same after that moment. If we follow the Biblical narrative further, we find the Bible depicts a fallen world, where sin is in the very fabric of life—all life. We now must live in a world where sin and futility are embedded in nature. In this sense, then, I argue that nothing we experience in this life is purely by God's design. Whatever utopia existed in the perfectly designed Garden no longer exists. That ship has sailed! What sense does it make, then, to impose utopian ideals onto our present reality?

What we can say, in light of the Garden narrative, is that all sexuality is now less than ideal, in the sense that nothing we experience now can compare to God's perfect design in the Garden. This applies to both the male and female binary and LGBTQ relationships—all of humanity is less than the ideal relationship found in the Garden of Eden narrative. Adam and Eve had no clothes, no pain, no abuse, no shame, and no guilt. There are in fact many things that God did not create in the Garden. While it is true that Steve is not in the Garden story, it is also true that many kinds of people are not in the Garden story. For example, grandparents, children and cousins are not mentioned. People born with abnormal conditions such as autism are not mentioned in the Garden. Where did such people come from? How was the earth populated from just two people without incest and inbreeding? Such questions expose the limitation of the Garden story. Stating that homosexuality is wrong merely because such a thing is not present in the Garden of Eden narrative is to stretch that narrative well beyond its teaching ability. What is more, we are hard-pressed to use the Garden story to support any of the sides of the LGBTQ discussion. When we attempt to make the Adam and Eve story our guide for sexual morality, we take the story to places it was never intended to go.

However, the Garden of Eden does teach some important lessons that I see as being entirely relevant to the gay debates. One lesson is that God is still working. God rested on the seventh day, so the story goes, but God did not stop creating entirely. We see so many other wonderful creations occurring after the original design, and none of them is considered wrong or sinful. Might not gender plurality be part of this new creation?

One important teaching the Garden of Eden story has for us is not about who is in the story, but about who is at center stage. The Lord God walked among the Garden, in addition to Adam and Eve. This God created both the man and the woman in his own image. This story, then, teaches an important truth that would help the church of our generation immensely. If the Lord God created certain human beings in a certain way, who are we to judge them as not worthy?

Furthermore, a critical teaching from the Garden is that the image of God is not dependent upon gender. Both the male and the female have the full image of God in them. They are both created in the image of God and neither the male nor the female is any more or any less made in the image of God. From the beginning, gender has no impact on whether a person is made in the image of God. One grand correction I suggest our

American church ought to make is to see all human beings, regardless of gender, as having the spark of the divine in them. Human beings, regardless of gender, deserve the chance to find their suitable helper.

## MALE AND FEMALE IN THE LAW

The trajectory of the "male and female" thread that begins in Genesis continues in the books of the Law. In particular, the concept of a male and female binary (as opposed to gender pluralism, which recognizes multiple genders beyond pure male and pure female) is expressed in the books of Leviticus and Deuteronomy. I suggest we look at how the Law viewed males and females, and realize that whatever perfect ideals about men and women we find in the Garden of Eden; such ideals are already lost by the time the Law was written. The "male and female" language of the Law is enlightening, to say the least. Two terms that accurately describe the Law's language are gender hierarchy and patriarchal dominance. Men are valued more highly than women. Men are dominant. Slaves are allowed. Multiple wives are allowed. The tone is clearly patriarchal in nature.

For example, the Law teaches this hierarchy rather clearly: "If the person is from a month old up to five years old, the valuation shall be for a male five shekels of silver, and for a female the valuation shall be three shekels of silver." (Leviticus 27:6)

The patriarchal and even polygamous nature of the gendered language in the Law is made clear in Deuteronomy as well. In chapter 17, verse 17, we read that a man must not "acquire many wives for himself" but there is no requirement to have only one wife. Then in chapter 21, verse 15 we read precepts for how to handle the inheritance of a man with two wives. The Law prescribes guidance for such a situation and what to do if a man loved one wife, but not the other. The Law does not condemn polygamy outright, but merely tempers the practice.

# UNCIRCUMCISED

Again, we see male dominant language and gender hierarchy embedded in the Law. These gender constructs contradict the utopian relationship found in the Garden of Eden story. Therefore, even God's own Law acknowledges that God's design for men and women found in the Garden of Eden are not necessary to have a God-approved society.

This ancient, God-approved society described in the Law no longer exists. And while there are Christians who would try to rebuild such a society, by and large the consensus among Christians is that we are to build a better society than that found in the Law. We are to build a "city on a hill". This puts my non-affirming friends in a tough position. If we are attempting to build a better society, a new Jerusalem, why do we seek guidance from the old Law? Furthermore, if we are looking to the Law for guidance in the matter of LGBTQ relationships, then we are going to have to begin living under the Law entirely. Thus, we would then need another Savoir to fulfill the Law all over again.

I ask, as Paul the Apostle asks, to those who want to live under the law of Moses, even in one matter, do you know what that law says? (Galatians 4:21) Do you realize that breaking one small part of that law means you have broken the entire covenant? Living under the Law was once a blessing and lead to a certain kind of society. Such a lifestyle, after the cross of Jesus, is now a curse. To build a society with guidance from the law of Moses is to contradict the work of the cross: "For all who rely on works of the law are under a curse; for it is written, 'Cursed be everyone who does not abide by all things written in the Book of the Law, and do them.'" (Galatians 3:10).

Now we get to the heart of the matter. One of the root questions uncovered by the so-called gay debates is this: Do we submit to the Law and build a society under the guidance of the Law? I have no better answer to this question than the answer Apostle Paul gives us:

> "Now before faith came, we were held captive under the law, imprisoned until the coming faith would be revealed. So

*then, the law was our guardian until Christ came, in order that we might be justified by faith. But now that faith has come, we are no longer under a guardian, for in Christ Jesus you are all sons of God, through faith."* (Galatians 3:23-26)

The gospel does not involve a submission to the law of Moses. If we claim to have obtained new power in Jesus to obey the law of Moses, we are deceived. If we claim our LGBTQ friends and family just need to pray more and wait for God's power to obey more perfectly, we deny entire books of the Bible, such as Hebrews, which say the love of Jesus is superior to the law of Moses. Such a gospel is circular in nature. If the cross freed us from the Law and its regulations, how can the good news be that we submit all over again to that same Law?

My contention is that the church will be forever divided over this issue unless we drop the message that the gospel is new power to submit to the Law. The Law was a guardian for those to whom it was given. The Spirit however is our new guardian.

## THREE KINDS OF EUNUCHS

If the two-gender construct of male and female is in fact essential to the Christian gospel, then we must look more closely at those who originated this gospel. Did Jesus, Paul, Peter, John and the others have any concept outside the realm of male and female? Did they present gender binary conformance as part of the gospel message? To begin answering these questions, I look to the topic of eunuchs in the Bible.

My point here is not that eunuchs are homosexuals, or vice versa. My point is to answer the question, did the Bible authors, and Jesus himself, have any kind of understanding, even remotely, that human sexuality and gender is more than purely male and female? Did they have the concept that non-male-and-female people exist and could have valid roles in society? I understand the ancient world had limited understanding of the plethoric array of concepts being debated in our generation.

# UNCIRCUMCISED

Still I contend that Matthew chapter 19 provides some insight.

> "And Pharisees came up to him and tested him by asking, 'Is it lawful to divorce one's wife for any cause?' He answered, 'Have you not read that he who created them from the beginning made them male and female, and said, 'Therefore a man shall leave his father and his mother and hold fast to his wife, and the two shall become one flesh'?" (Matthew 19:3-6)

What I see here is Jesus responding to an outrageous question, meant to be a trap, with a slap in the face. My shorthand summary of this passage is this. Can we divorce for any reason? No. Does God love divorce? No. Does divorce happen? Yes. In other words, Jesus is saying, "stuff happens". Moses allowed divorce. God does not like divorce but it happens. In a post-utopian world where the Garden of Eden no longer exists, we must deal with the fact that divorce happens, and at times divorce is the right course of action. What I hear Jesus saying here in this passage is kind of like this: "Don't be stupid! If you want a place where there is no divorce, go back to Eden!"

On a more convicting note, Jesus is teaching faithfulness here. In contrast to the fanciful question that sparked this teaching, Jesus teaches faithfulness. (Matthew 19:7-9)

These verses should cause us to pause for a moment. When we present our LGBTQ affirming ideas, are we communicating them like the Pharisees in this passage? If we communicate an anything-goes, throw-morality-out-the-window message, we should not be surprised by the strong reaction from those who hold non-affirming positions. Jesus has strong, God's-design arguments in response to wild immorality. Sooner rather than later, we ought to realize that we need both the liberal and the conservative viewpoints about sin, gender, and marriage. Such a bond of views would be a brave new world, and I suggest we who are affirming do not need to fear such a world. Every hard teaching of Jesus is laced with mercy, forgiveness, and joy.

> *The disciples said to him, "If such is the case of a man with his wife, it is better not to marry." But he said to them, "Not everyone can receive this saying, but only those to whom it is given. For there are eunuchs who have been so from birth, and there are eunuchs who have been made eunuchs by men, and there are eunuchs who have made themselves eunuchs for the sake of the kingdom of heaven. Let the one who is able to receive this receive it." (Matthew 19:10-12)*

The disciples react just as some do today. Some pastors say that if society allows same-sex marriage, then we should just get rid of marriage all together. Other pastors are joining together to only ordain traditional male and female marriages, and only if they are already Christians.

Rather than take our toys and go home, I see a far more Christ-like response here. Some teachings we can glean from this passage: Jesus says not everyone can accept the Garden of Eden perfection. Jesus mentions three types of people who did not marry in society: Some do not marry because of their birth, some do not marry because of their situation, and some do not marry because of their choice.

While eunuchs do not exactly equate to homosexuals, we should be asking some challenging questions to those who point to these verses in the Bible to justify excluding our LGBTQ friends and family from marriage. Is Jesus giving us a systematic guide for creating marriage theology here? I see such a path as deviating from the textual intent. To create a non-affirming theology from these verses is a bastardization of the text. On the other hand, to use the eunuch passages as justification for affirming same-sex marriage is also a bastardization of the text. I find it far healthier then to simply acknowledge three primary teachings from this Matthew 19 story: Jesus understood there are people who exist outside the male and female binary, marriage is about faithfulness, and finally, accepting male and female marriage is not a requirement for being a Christ follower.

# UNCIRCUMCISED

## NO MALE AND FEMALE

Where does the trajectory of "male and female" end up in the Bible? I see the conclusion of this trajectory in Galatians. Specifically, Galatians 3:28 sums up the teaching: "There is neither Jew nor Greek, there is neither slave nor free, there is no male and female, for you are all one in Christ Jesus." A similar teaching is found in Colossians 3: "Here there is not Greek and Jew, circumcised and uncircumcised, barbarian, Scythian, slave, free; but Christ is all, and in all." (Colossians 3:11).

I find these to be profound statements that should influence our debates. In the end, gender must not be a dividing issue in the church. There is no male and female. This point is underscored by Jesus himself. When asked about the resurrection, Jesus taught a remarkable lesson: "For in the resurrection they neither marry nor are given in marriage, but are like angels in heaven." Matthew 22:30 (ESV) There will be no gender or marriage in heaven because, like the angels, we will be genderless. If such a condition is the ultimate end of our existence, so the teaching goes, why then do we make gender such a dividing issue in this life?

When we revisit the Bible with this male and female trajectory in mind, we see numerous passages illuminated in new ways. For example, we can now see quite a few gender-bending stories previously passed over. As I already mentioned, the first person officially witnessed to in the book of Acts was not male or female, but a eunuch. In the story of David and Jonathan, what does it mean that David loved Jonathan more than women? (2 Samuel 1:26) Why did the author use the word "cling", a word with sexual overtones, to describe Ruth's relationship with Naomi? (Ruth 1:6-18) Why does the Bible honor the gender-twisting role of Deborah, who was judging and leading in a man's role? (Judges 4:4)

The illumination continues in the New Testament writings. What was the relationship between the Centurion and his "pais" in Matthew 8:5-13, and can we assume this relationship was non-sexual, contrary to almost all other such Roman relationships at the time? What if Jesus blessed them regardless of their relationship?

One of my favorite verses to bring up in regard to gender-bending passages in the Bible is the repeated command to great each other with a holy kiss. Why do we not greet each other with a holy kiss at church? (1 Corinthians 16:20) My point in raising these gender-bending verses is not to prove they support affirmation of our LGBTQ friends and family, but to demonstrate the fact that the Bible, as a whole, is not so clear about promoting a male and female only society. In fact, what I see in the Bible is a marvelously progressive teaching.

In the Garden of Eden (e.g. Genesis 5), we see a perfect gender binary presented. In the Law (e.g. Leviticus 25), we see an unequal gender binary being supported. In the teachings of Jesus, we see a contested or overlooked gender binary (e.g. Matthew 19, Matthew 22). Finally, in the kingdom of God presented by the New Testament writers, we see a superseded gender binary, where citizens of this spiritual kingdom are exhorted to both avoid sexual immorality and to not generate hostility regarding gender (Galatians 3, Colossians 3, Acts 8).

**UNCIRCUMCISED**

# MARRIAGE... AND SUITABILITY

*"Then the Lord God said, 'It is not good that the man should be alone; I will make him a helper fit for him.'"*
- Genesis 2:18 ESV

When the topic of marriage surfaces in the gay debates, things get weird and a double standard arises. In a typical American church, heterosexual people are held to a standard of purity mixed with mercy. However, our LGBTQ friends and family are often held to a standard of purity void of mercy, where all passion and all desire of a sexual nature are demanded to be crucified. Such a heavy burden is too much for many LGBTQ youth, and dire consequences ensure. What my affirming friends and I are requesting from the American church is not a relaxation or abandonment of sexual purity, but equal treatment of all people regardless of their current sexual identity. So while I agree with exhortations such as Galatians 5:24 to "crucify the flesh", I seek the corrective in the American church to apply these exhortations for purity in a consistent manner. Why does keeping your passions in check require LGBTQ friends and family to live in a locked closet, hiding their sexual nature? Such hypocritical teachings from the American church have disastrous effects for those who are not part of the pure male and female binary structure of society.

In addition to revealing inconsistent teachings in the American church, the so-call gay debates also reveal the critical role marriage plays in the American church, both Protestant and Catholic. In fact, marriage theology is at the heart and soul of Christianity in America. We who affirm same-sex marriage should not be too surprised at all the ruckus stirred up by church-going American Christians. To affirm same-sex marriage is to challenge the very core of Christian ideals in America.

For example, the First Things journal, published by The Institute on Religion and Public Life, has much to say about the importance of marriage to Christianity. R.R. Reno writes this for the year 2017:

> "What we need in 2017 and beyond is a renewal of covenant, of the paradoxically empowering bondage of loves and loyalties we gratefully affirm. Faith's covenant with the divine is most important. It anchors our communities of faith. Next is the covenant of marriage, which gives stability to domestic life. In the middle is our civic covenant, the affective union that puts the solidity into solidarity." --First Things In The Year Ahead, 12/30/2016.

While most Christians could agree on faith being the most important value, why is marriage the second most important value? This stands in stark contrast to what I read in the Bible. Somewhere in the last 500 years or so, perhaps since Luther's reforming nail, marriage theology has taken center stage. Perhaps we can look to Pope John Paul II, and his book, Theology of the Body. Or maybe the rise of marriage theology can be attributed to the Second Vatican Council in 1965, where the council devotes an entire section (Pastoral Constitution Gaudium) to family, marriage, and how specific marriage constructs are godly.

In my brief but revealing research into Christian church history, I find little evidence of the emphasis on the centrality of marriage to Christianity before recent centuries. Marriage is important to Christianity, to be sure, but when did marriage become the dominant theological construct by which Christians are marked, second only to divine faith? Christians have typically been marked by sexual purity, but not necessarily always by marriage. I would surmise the reason for widespread obsession with sexuality among American Christians could be due to this binding of holiness and theology with marriage.

We are experiencing a church in America who promotes "one man, one woman marriage" as the Christian ideal, and in fact bound to the gospel. This message is being sent so strongly by the American churches that Christians are known simply as "anti-gay". Pastors are getting fired up about opposing same-sex marriage, to say the least.

One trend that has arisen among Christian pastors is to abstain from marriage altogether. Some are withdrawing their marriage services, no longer participating in the signing of State certificates of marriage for anyone, straight, gay or otherwise. It seems they are taking their toys and going home. Others are only providing marriages for those who fit their criteria for a Christian marriage. As I write these words, already 786 church leaders have taken the First Things marriage pledge online. Here is an excerpt from the pledge that shows just how passionate the American church is about marriage theology:

> *"Therefore, in our roles as Christian ministers, we, the undersigned, commit ourselves to disengaging civil and Christian marriage in the performance of our pastoral duties. We will no longer serve as agents of the state in marriage. We will no longer sign government-provided marriage certificates. We will ask couples to seek civil marriage separately from their church-related vows and blessings. We will preside only at those weddings that seek to establish a Christian marriage in accord with the principles articulated and lived out from the beginning of the Church's life."*

Such a pledge begs many questions. What is a Christian marriage? Who qualifies? What kind of witness does this send to society?

# UNCIRCUMCISED

## THE PURPOSE OF MARRIAGE

Before things get too out of hand and the American church closes its doors to all non-Christians any further, I suggest the church revisit the Christian purpose of marriage. I know the church can do this, because it has done it already. Not too long ago, marriage was more of a land contract than a personal contract. If a man bought land with a woman on it, she became his wife, and often was part of the exchange for the land. The church worked to change this. Even more recently, interracial marriages were strongly discouraged by the American church, until the church realized its mistake. Repeatedly, the church has gotten the purpose marriage misconstrued, and then corrected itself. Might we make another correction to the marriage contract?

Seeing the contradictions in picking only part of the Law to support the non-affirming position and deny marriage to LGBTQ friends and family, my non-affirming friends move on to the most common argument I hear about marriage, that is, the procreation argument. The thought is that the marriage covenant requires procreation. If you get married, then you must have children. I find this a contradictory definition of the purpose of marriage. If we promote the argument that marriage has a procreation requirement, then we have put ourselves in a precarious situation. How would couples who cannot bear children fit into marriage? Are they now banned from marriage? What about those who once could have children but now cannot, perhaps due to an accident of some kind? Are they now no longer married? Suppose an 80-year-old couple want to get married. There will be no children in their future, yet the church would likely not refuse their marriage vows. The basis of all these kinds of marriages is clearly the love between the two people. The purpose of marriage must be about more than procreation, and might not even include procreation at all.

My claim is that we ought to revisit what the Bible has to say about marriage, give marriage proper respect, and stop elevating marriage to gospel status. Not a single verse in the

Bible, that I can find, binds marriage as a part of the gospel messages. Today's church, then, in my mind, has wrongly made an idol out of marriage. Instead of stubbornly holding onto a specific variant of marriage, I suggest we make yet another adjustment to the marriage purpose to include all of humanity and the entire spectrum of sexuality that exists.

Throughout the Bible, we in fact see multiple, shifting purposes of marriage. Rather than defining marriage universally, the Bible seems to reflect society's definitions of marriage. For example, as I just pointed out, the Bible authors are not bothered by things like polygamy. Here is a brief survey of what I find about the purpose of marriage in the Bible: The common theme I find about marriage in the Bible is that the contract is about faithfulness (Hebrews 13:4). Marriage is a concession and not a mandate. Marriage not a requirement for all people (Matthew 19:10-11; 1 Corinthians 7:1-5). Marriage is a safe place for procreation, but does not require procreation, for being childless is not a curse (Psalm 113:9) Marriage is about kinship bonds (Matthew 19:4-6), about companionship (Genesis 2:18-24), and is a gift to be honored as a good thing (Proverbs 18:22). Most remarkably, Jesus himself teaches that marriage will not exist in heaven (Matthew 22:30).

In the end, I find the best definition of the purpose of marriage in Genesis. Genesis 2:18 reads, "Then the Lord God said, 'It is not good that the man should be alone; I will make him a helper fit for him.'" The purpose of marriage, as I read it, is to fill the void of emptiness. Not everyone has such a void, but it is a common human characteristic to need a "fit helper", one suited to help the other—a true companion. In this line of thought, I ask, who is a suitable helper to a lesbian? Is it not another lesbian? It could be. Alternatively, perhaps in certain situations, it is not another lesbian. My point is that in regard to marriage, we ought to step back and give people the freedom to find out what is the most suitable situation for themselves. If two gay men find they are fit for each other, and fill the void of loneliness in each other, why should the church refuse their marriage vows? Why would we undo what God has brought together?

I contend the Bible does not elevate marriage to the supreme status today's American church gives it. Such attitudes toward marriage are not limited to the Protestant churches. Pope John Paul's Roman Catholic book, *The Theology of the Body*, drastically blurs the lines between human sexuality and the concept of the body of Christ found in the Bible. For the sake of guarding Godly marriages, have we opened the door to toxic, rationalized abuse? Why do some forbid or despise certain kinds of marriages, such as interracial marriages? My thought is that our Christian witness can be vastly improved when we stop protecting what we call the sanctity of marriage and start looking for the goodness around us. What God has joined together is good. Examples of LGBTQ marriages abound in America and around the world. And they are good.

As a case in point, I share the story of Eli and Don, who are friends of a friend of mine:

> "We met online in a dating site, we were about 50 miles apart. After chatting online and on the phone we decided to meet in person. We fell in love with each other instantly. After that, we would see each other on a weekly basis. The more we spent time together the closer we got. Despite our age difference, we dated for about a year but nothing serious. On February 14th, we decided to commit without knowing what the future would have in store for us."
>
> Following that, a few weeks later, Don had an accident that put him in a wheelchair. I visited him as much as I could at the hospital and at the rehab center, but he didn't have anybody to come home to. I was having issues with my own family and I had been thrown out of the house.
>
> After I gathered my things and left, I called Don and told him what happened. I said "I don't know where I'm headed but I will let you know" "Come home," he replied. I got to Don's house before they brought him home from the hospital, and I was waiting with a smile. That was April 19th, 2009.

*It was hard at first because I never been on my own but I could feel that I was in the right place, next to him. We got involved with the LGBT community about 2 years after living together and have been involved since then. We always talked about one day being able to get married. We discussed about having a Holy Union. In 2015, there was talk about gay marriage becoming legalized. So we made plans to go to Florida and do it there. But the same-sex marriage law in America passed while we were in Alabama, and so we went and got hitched here in our home state, along other couples. We felt loved with our friends and surrounded by our community."*

Why does the church see itself as the guardian of marriage? Whether it is forbidding interracial marriages, interfaith marriages or same-sex marriages, the church has often seen itself as the guardian of marriage. I ask, what are we protecting? Do we have any evidence to show that our marriages have been sanctified by guarding one-man, one-woman, same-faith, same-race marriage? The evidence I have seen shows hypocrisy, not success. We used to declare that interracial marriages were not blessed. Then we declared interfaith marriages were not blessed. Now we say same-sex marriages are not blessed. Each time, it is love that overcame all this forbidding of marriage. Love like that shared between Eli and Don is eternal. I contend we Christians are on thin ice when we dismiss such profound love. Rather than forbid LGBTQ people from marriage, I suggest the Christian church give people freedom to marry or not to marry, and to marry whom they want.

## THE CHOICE OF CELIBACY

In stark contrast to marriage, which is a covenant that has been changed many times in church history, celibacy is a covenant that has not been modified throughout the 2,000-year history of the Christian church. Celibacy has been presented as a gift and a choice that rests on each person who makes the choice to remain celibate. Yet the current church would have us completely modify the celibacy covenant. While the definition of temporary celibacy, more accurately called abstinence, has changed from generation to generation, celibacy has been seen as a lifelong calling.

In 1 Corinthians chapter 7, we see Paul's discourse on marriage and celibacy. His purpose is clearly not to give God's commands about such things, but to share his advice: "Now concerning the betrothed, I have no command from the Lord, but I give my judgment as one who by the Lord's mercy is trustworthy." (1 Corinthians 7:25). What is more, Paul's utmost concern is not to put restraints upon the church: "I say this for your own benefit, not to lay any restraint upon you, but to promote good order and to secure your undivided devotion to the Lord." (1 Corinthians 7:34)

How wonderful today's church could be if we followed such a pattern! Today's church instead lays down a heavy restraint on believers, exhorting us to bind a specific version of marriage with the gospel and enforcing celibacy as a mandate for our LGBTQ friends and family.

Celibacy is a witness of God's love, even more so than marriage. It pains me to see marriage elevated as the highest form of love when historically celibacy has been properly seen as a higher calling. Sadly, the church of today misses the point of celibacy entirely. Instead of a grand blessing and example of Christ, celibacy has become the "go-to" solution for non-affirming Christians. They have to give some option to gays. Since marriage and promiscuity are off the table, celibacy is the only option left for non-affirming Christians. Celibacy is a gift. When mandated as a requirement for Christian life however, celibacy becomes enslavement. I contend the church must look elsewhere, beyond celibacy, for the model of how to interact with our LGBTQ friends and family.

## THE BRIDE NARRATIVE

The real reason today's church is so infatuated with marriage theology may be something known as the Bride narrative. Those familiar with the Bible will readily recognize these stories. All four Gospel writings, Matthew, Mark, Luke, and John, mention the Bride stories. There are three such stories that I find in the Bible.

One Bride narrative is found in Jesus' answer to those who criticized his disciples for not following the legalistic demands of the Law: "And Jesus said to them, "Can the wedding guests mourn as long as the bridegroom is with them? The days will come when the bridegroom is taken away from them, and then they will fast." (Matthew 9:15) The teaching, given by Jesus, is allegorical imagery where Jesus is the bridegroom and the disciples are wedding guests. This kind of identification has taken center stage in American theological systems. Such identification speaks into the narrative of privilege, the idea that Christians are special and blessed. I find this both amusing and sad, since the point Jesus is making is to counteract the special, blessed, privileged self-identification of the Pharisees due to their fasting and praying.

The second Bride narrative is Jesus' teaching about ten virgins waiting on a bridegroom, found in Matthew 25:1-2: "Then the kingdom of heaven will be like ten virgins who took their lamps and went to meet the bridegroom. Five of them were foolish, and five were wise." Again, the imagery is that Jesus is the bridegroom, but now there is a twist. The disciples are not guests, but virgin girls. My non-affirming friends who tend to take the Bible literally suddenly stop doing so when confronted with these verses. They switch their Bible approach to a more liberal, progressive interpretation to avoid being labeled as virgin girls!

The third Bride narrative is found in Revelations. "Let us rejoice and exult and give him the glory, for the marriage of the Lamb has come, and his Bride has made herself ready;" (Revelation 19:7) The picture presented here is that the church is the Bride of Jesus. This further builds on Jesus' image of himself as the bridegroom.

Entire theological systems of thought have been developed around these three Bride narratives. I find this most peculiar, since allegories and parables are literary constructs with limited meaning. Taking an allegorical statement too far yields highly unpredictable results, and strays dearly from the author's original intentions. In my observation, this is precisely what we have done in the American church. We have extrapolated far too much meaning from the wonderful Bride stories in the Bible. We have gone beyond what was intended and added to what is written.

And for what purpose? We claim the Bride narratives are second only to faith in God so that we can prevent our LGBTQ family and friends from entering into marriage contracts that have potential for amazing blessing, goodness, and Christian witness of faithfulness and love. By doing so, we have turned our churches into toxic halls lined with eggshells.

I find solace in pastor Andy Stanley's thoughts.

> *"We just need to decide from now on in our churches when a Middle School kid comes out to his small group leader or a high school young lady comes out to her parents,"* he said. *"We just need to decide, regardless of what you think about this topic — no more students are going to feel like they have to leave the local church because they're same-sex attracted or because they're gay. That ends with us."* Andy emphasizes the church should be the *"safest place on the planet for students to talk about anything, including same-sex attraction."* (Pastor Andy Stanley, Christianity Today, 4/20/2015)

## NO MARRIAGE

The marriage teachings in the Bible find their culmination in Jesus' profound statement in response to a wild, morbid question about marriage posed by some teachers of the law.

> "And the seven left no offspring. Last of all the woman also died. In the resurrection, when they rise again, whose wife will she be? For the seven had her as wife." (Mark 12:22-23)

Jesus minces no words in response. "Is this not the reason you are wrong, because you know neither the Scriptures nor the power of God? For when they rise from the dead, they neither marry nor are given in marriage, but are like angels in heaven. And as for the dead being raised, have you not read in the book of Moses, in the passage about the bush, how God spoke to him, saying,

> 'I am the God of Abraham, and the God of Isaac, and the God of Jacob'? He is not God of the dead, but of the living. You are quite wrong." (Mark 12:24-27)

I contend today's American church is quite wrong about same-sex marriage. There will be no gender or marriage in heaven

> "For in the resurrection they neither marry nor are given in marriage, but are like angels in heaven." (Matthew 29:30)

Whatever truths God wants to communicate through the metaphor between Christ and His Bride have been lost or obfuscated in the church. I think that the metaphor can be renewed best by welcoming same-sex marriages, which teach us to move beyond sex and to think about companionship, faithfulness, love, empathy and equality. The suitable helper teaching in Genesis 2 shines brightly in same-sex marriages. Should not every human being have the freedom to find a suitable helper? Who is more suitable to a lesbian than another lesbian? Who is more suitable than the one you love most?

# UNCIRCUMCISED

My claim is that by guarding and protecting a narrow definition of marriage, the church will eventually destroy the Bride metaphor. What relationship does the Bride have with Jesus our Lord if we use sex as our primary image in the metaphor? Should we not move beyond sex and speak about the companionship and help that should be in all our relationships? The conversation should move beyond marriage itself. Why protect marriage so desperately, as if the entire future of the church depended on it when clearly the future has nothing to do with marriage?

# UNCIRCUMCISED
WELCOMING LGBTQ PEOPLE INTO THE FAMILY OF GOD

UNCIRCUMCISED

# HOLINESS... AND LAW

*"For in Christ Jesus neither circumcision nor uncircumcision counts for anything, but only faith working through love."*

*- Galatians 5:6 ESV*

One of the primary reasons I affirm our LGBTQ friends and family as they are, without any need to change their sexuality, is because I have revisited the idea of holiness. I affirm the gender plurality we see in humanity not only because God is love, but also because God is holy. Let me explain.

In the Old Covenant, holiness is defined as keeping yourself and your community clean in specific ways. Precept after precept in the old Law is about cleanliness and uncleanliness. To be holy, then, is often preached in American churches as being clean—clean in our speech, our actions, our sexuality, our prayers, and on and on. For many years of Bible study and regular religious service, I did not question this idea that holiness means cleanliness and purity. The so-called gay debates changed all that.

Examining holiness more carefully in the Bible reveals two definitions, an old one and a really old one. The New Covenant tells us Law-based holiness has been fulfilled by Jesus who is the Christ, and takes us back to the original definition of holiness—righteousness credited by faith.

When Jesus taught about holiness, his teaching turned Law-based holiness upside down. Jesus taught that holiness is not about keeping yourself clean, but about your willingness to be unclean for the sake of serving your neighbor, your enemy, and anyone you encounter. Because your faith already makes you clean, you are free to do good. It is no longer how clean we are, but how good we are, that determines our judgment from God. That is how it was with Abraham, whose faith was credited to him as righteousness. And it is what Jesus teaches.

When Jesus described the final, holy judgement, how did he describe that judgment? When the Son of Man comes in his glory, and all the angels with him, and he sits on his glorious throne, the criteria of judgment is this:

> *"Come, you who are blessed by my Father, inherit the kingdom prepared for you from the foundation of the world. For I was hungry and you gave me food, I was thirsty and you gave me drink, I was a stranger and you welcomed me, I was naked and you clothed me, I was sick and you visited me, I was in prison and you came to me." (Matthew 25:34-36)*

The criteria here has nothing to do with how clean you are; judgement is about how dirty you are willing to get in order to feed, welcome, clothe, and visit other people.

This is a serious thought that should send shock waves through every pulpit in America. Why do we spend so much effort to keep ourselves clean when the final judgment is about serving other people? A prison is not exactly a clean place. The street is not a place free of temptation. Shelters for the poor tend to be filled with dirty people. To be holy is to go to such unclean places and care for the people who are there.

This definition of holiness is seen throughout the teachings of Jesus and the writings of the New Covenant authors. For example, consider the story about Peter, the primary disciple taught by Jesus, found in Acts 10:

> *"The next day, as they were on their journey and approaching the city, Peter went up on the housetop about the sixth hour to pray. And he became hungry and wanted something to eat, but while they were preparing it, he fell*

*into a trance and saw the heavens opened and something like a great sheet descending, being let down by its four corners upon the earth. In it were all kinds of animals and reptiles and birds of the air. And there came a voice to him: 'Rise, Peter; kill and eat.' But Peter said, 'By no means, Lord; for I have never eaten anything that is common or unclean.' And the voice came to him again a second time, 'What God has made clean, do not call common.' This happened three times, and the thing was taken up at once to heaven."* (Acts 10:9-16)

In the Old Covenant, these animals in Peter's dream are unclean. To eat such reptiles and birds of the air would be an abomination to Peter and his Law-based mind. Even three and a half years of teaching directly from Jesus did not remove the old definition of holiness. To Peter, holiness meant to be clean based on God's codes of cleanliness. As the story continues, God teaches Peter the new definition of holiness: to go and visit those once considered unclean, for they are now called clean by God. (Acts 10:17-20)

The dream Peter had about eating unclean animals really had nothing to do with the dietary laws of the Old Covenant. The teaching is to go with the three men looking for him. Peter was to go and visit a whole bunch of people, Gentiles, who had been considered unclean in the Old Covenant definition of holiness. Now however, these Gentiles were clean! They were still Gentiles, just as the reptiles were still reptiles. God has declared a new definition of holiness, and it is not about keeping yourself pure. Holiness is about serving the needs of those once called unclean. Holiness is about visiting our family, our friends, our neighbors, and even our enemies. Have you visited your LGBTQ family or friends?

## RESPECTING CONSCIENCE

One of the important components of holiness is the concept of conscience. Often the Bible authors wrote about the importance having a clean conscience yourself and about respecting the conscience of others. To respect the conscience of other people is a sorely needed corrective in the American church. I find this corrective is needed on both sides of the so-called gay debates. Are we paying attention to the conscience of those we debate? "Thus, sinning against your brothers and wounding their conscience when it is weak, you sin against Christ." (1 Corinthians 8:12)

In my reading of the Bible, I find this idea of respecting other people's consciences being central to the resolution of hostility in the first century church caused by the circumcision debates. How did the first church resolve the hostility between the conscience that demanded circumcision as a requirement for salvation and the conscience that saw no need for literal circumcision demanded by the Law?

Peter, James, and John were in the pro-circumcision camp. Paul, Titus, and Barnabas were in the anti-circumcision camp. Their consciences seem mutually exclusive, given the stunning clarity of God's Law in the Bible. The story of how they finally came together in one mind is found in Galatians 2.

> *"On the contrary, when they saw that I had been entrusted with the gospel to the uncircumcised, just as Peter had been entrusted with the gospel to the circumcised (for he who worked through Peter for his apostolic ministry to the circumcised worked also through me for mine to the Gentiles), and when James and Cephas and John, who seemed to be pillars, perceived the grace that was given to me, they gave the right hand of fellowship to Barnabas and me, that we should go to the Gentiles and they to the circumcised. Only, they asked us to remember the poor, the very thing I was eager to do." (Galatians 2:7-10)*

What an astonishing event! Those who were convinced God's Law demanded circumcision for Christians gave the right hand of fellowship to those who said circumcision was not necessary for salvation. Peter, James, and John let their conscience unbind from the Law and extended the right hand of fellowship to Paul, Titus, and Barnabas. This is what must happen in the debates about LGBTQ people. Hostility will reign until our consciences unbind from the Law and respect the grace found in the conscience of others.

It is highly notable here, that no one's conscience promoted unfaithfulness, bitterness, impurity, or uncleanliness of any kind. These Christians let go of the Law's demands but they did not let go of holiness. Because of the gospel of grace and for the sake of compassion for the poor and needy, they united as one people.

Those who added requirements to faith were the ones who bore the burden of extending the right hand of fellowship to those who claimed pure freedom in Christ because of the grace of God on the cross.

Those who are affirming ought to have more respect for the non-affirming conscience. By affirming same-sex marriage we are not merely asking the non-affirmer to accept our sense of love and justice, we are demanding that they restructure their entire theological worldview. We should not be surprised at the strong reactions we often experience. Nor should we be surprised at how long it may take to come to an affirming stance. In everything, we ought to bear with the conscience of one another with patience.

I am convinced that such holy respect for the conscience of our neighbor and even our enemy will come from the LGBTQ community. As I listen to more and more authentic self-narratives and experiences of gay people, transgender people and queer people, I am even more enlightened to respect the conscience of other people.

There are gay people who are convicted to stay celibate. There are gay people who desire to marry. There are transgender people who seek to express their suppressed gender that does not match their biological gender. There are queer, bisexual and intersexual people who want to figure themselves out in a safe place. There are straight people who empathize with gender and sexual outliers but do not know how to interact with them. There are non-affirming people who cannot welcome gender and sexual outliers at this time. Does not love demand us to respect each other? Could not the Christian church be the example of such respect? Might we give people breathing room to figure out the tangled web of gender identity and sexual orientation without fear and punishment?

## PROMOTING PURITY

"Clean, or not clean?" That is the question often posed by the holiness laws found in the commands and precepts given to Moses. When I read the priestly duties found in the section of the Bible called Leviticus, the entire job of the priest seems to be to determine whether a person is clean or unclean. Such cleanliness laws include sexual behavior and represent a rather limited understanding of the human body. Menstruation, for example, is said to make a woman unclean and ejaculation is said to make a man unclean.

Does today's American church follow such cleanliness laws? Do we hear Christians promoting purity based on this kind of holiness? Apart from a few extremists, the answer is no, the church no longer promotes purity based on the Bible's Old Covenant holiness laws. Why is this?

We no longer see a need to obey the cleanliness laws primarily because of the teaching of Jesus and the apostles. Jesus broke down the hostility between unclean lepers and the religious society when Jesus touched a leper after delivering the Sermon on the Mount (Matthew 8). Peter's vision of unclean animals and being told to eat the unclean animals in his vision paved a clear path for future Christians to set aside the commands in the Bible about determining purity. Unclean animals became religiously clean, and available for food. Unclean people, such as lepers, became religiously clean, and available to be helped.

Our Christian conscious is not bothered, for the most part, by disobeying God's Biblical commands about cleanliness, whether the commands are in regard to animals or people.

Tim Otto makes this point vividly clear in his book, *Oriented to Faith: Transforming the Conflict over Gay Relationships.*

> "We no longer go through rites of purification after ejaculating or menstruating, for we realize that spiritual health is not about what goes in or out of orifices, but what comes out of the heart. Jesus taught us this when he said, 'It's not what goes into your mouth that defiles you; you are defiled by the words that come out of your mouth' (Matt 15: 11, NLT). So perhaps it is not the 'faggot' who is defiled, but rather the one who says 'faggot,' or similar slurs, with the intent to harm."

The purity and cleanliness components of holiness, for Christians, is not about following holiness codes or laws, but about improving our character and our speech. The guide for such improvement is the Holy Spirit. We are held accountable for growing in purity of speech and cleanliness of character by Christian community, our own conscience, and the guidance of more experienced Christians. Why then do some Christians immediately turn to the Old Covenant holiness codes as reason for excluding or limiting blessing on our LGBTQ friends and family? Do such people really want to go back to the days of having your wives and daughters sit in a purity tent in the backyard every month?

Setting aside this ironic hypocrisy for a moment, I can see a valid concern in the conscience of people who do look to the holiness codes when confronted by gender and sexual outliers. The concern, as I understand it, is about restraint. If we welcome and affirm LGBTQ people, how do we continue to speak against sin, abuse, and wrongdoing? If we allow same-sex marriage openly, how is our Christian faith any different from antinomianism, which supposes there is no law and that every person is free to act in any manner?

I have been accused of being an antinomian a few times, which means people sometimes see me as "the man of lawlessness". An antinomian is someone who believes that the grace of God renders moral law useless. The antinomian view is that moral law has no obligation because faith alone is necessary to salvation. Antinomians typically reject socially established morality. Is this what I am promoting?

I must admit that for a time, I had no idea how to incorporate holiness into my grace-alone theology. The following question haunted me for many nights: If we can see the breakdown of the "male and female" patriarchal system in our society… and if we agree that the gospel is the way through the wall of hostility between gays and the church…how do we avoid the charge of condoning all forms of immorality, fornication, and sinful behavior? How do we maintain moral fortitude with gospel consistency and at the same time affirm same-sex marriage?

I began incorporating the idea of purity and cleanliness into my theology by articulating actions I do not affirm. To be affirming of same-sex marriage does not mean to be affirming of all types of sexual behavior. I do not affirm abuse of others with sex. I do not affirm the excess of sexual activity or promiscuity. I do not affirm rape, prostitution, or pedophilia. I do not affirm adultery, polygamy, or incest. For generation after generation, Christians have been marked by a desire for purity, among other marks. I uphold this mark, even at the risk of adding yet another label to my theology, the label of being a prude. Like Jesus who was called a glutton and a drunkard (Matthew 11:19), I sometimes feel that I cannot win. Either I am an antinomian who throws out all morality or I am a prude who promotes too much morality. In the end, I accept all these labels and continue to work out my theology.

My breakthrough in regard to adding holiness into my theology came when I began reading the work of Richard Beck, author and professor of psychology at Abilene Christian University. His blog article, "On Love and the Yuck Factor", is nothing short of miraculous. Beck supposes that cleanliness, in the New Covenant, is not so much about keeping yourself pure and clean, but about how much you get dirty in order to help other people. Perhaps the most challenging roadblock for Christians to welcome and affirm LGBTQ people is our own sense of disgust. Perhaps we just think same-sex marriage is icky and yucky. And maybe, just maybe, that disgust is God's call to dive deeper and discover a more robust holiness.

## NO LAW

Can we find holiness without a holiness code telling us explicitly what is right and wrong? Many claim we cannot. They fear the slippery slope of falling into moral decay if we move away from God's Law (i.e. both the Ten Commandments and the 613 Torah regulations).

I contend differently, however. I stand with all those who have preached obedience to the Spirit—the Holy Spirit who now governs where the holiness codes of the Law once ruled. The Law of God had a purpose, but was only a foreshadow of things to come (Hebrews 10:1), was fulfilled on the cross (Colossians 2:13-15), no longer serves as our holiness supervisor (Galatians 3:25, Galatians 4:21), and is in fact obsolete and fading away (Hebrews 8:13). God is both love and holy. When we display the fruits of the Spirit, we find that against such things there is no law.

In the Sermon on the Mount, Jesus implores us to do one of the most troublesome, difficult acts anyone could ever do. Instead of a new law or new set of commands, Jesus gives his followers new principles, rooted in love.

> *"You have heard that it was said, 'You shall love your neighbor and hate your enemy.' But I say to you, Love your enemies and pray for those who persecute you, so that you may be sons of your Father who is in heaven. For he makes his sun rise on the evil and on the good, and sends rain on the just and on the unjust." (Matthew 5:43-45 )*

# UNCIRCUMCISED

To be godly, to be like God who shows love to everyone by sending sunshine and rain without favoritism, we are to love our enemy. We are to love other Christians. I am not going to claim to have any secrets as to how to do this. What I do know is that loving our enemy must be possible, and that doing so is one of the most incredible witnesses of love we have. Furthermore, love for enemies and love for one another is perhaps the single greatest distinctive of Christianity, and is not rooted in obedience to a law.

Regardless of how many times the church says "We love gays!" one thing is clear to those of us outside the church: LGBTQ people are seen by the church as the enemy. My claim is that instead of leading people to the law of Moses, we should be attracting people to the love of Jesus. When we welcome and affirm those we have once considered our enemies, we will open the door to become a beacon of godliness for the world.

# UNCIRCUMCISED
WELCOMING LGBTQ PEOPLE INTO THE FAMILY OF GOD

UNCIRCUMCISED

# TRUTH... AND QUESTIONS

> "Contrary to what some have led us to believe, a postmodern world is not one in which all order, meaning, and truth is lost. Rather, all that is lost is the kind of order, meaning, and truth that modernity had insisted upon. The good news of the postmodern gospel is that, with the end of modernity, we now have an ever-greater opportunity to order our lives, not based on an understanding of some universal, objective truth, but rather on an intimate understanding of a truth that is personal—indeed, a truth that is a person."
>
> - James Danaher,
> *Eyes That See, Ears That Hear:*
> *Perceiving Jesus in a Postmodern Context*

"You are rejecting the truth!" A common mischaracterization I encounter in the debates with those who take some form of non-affirming stance toward our LGBTQ friends and family is the claim that I am throwing out the truth of God. They further claim that I am ignoring the Bible. Such misplaced claims almost always spell the end of the discussions. My non-affirming acquaintances go away in silence. Rarely do I hear from them ever again. Hostility takes the form of uneasy silence and unhealthy tension.

What if there is a way through this hostility? Can the conversation continue? My claim is just that—the LGBTQ conversation can and must continue. If the truth will set us free, then we are compelled to keep asking questions until tension is resolved and relationships are repaired. Family bonds were

# UNCIRCUMCISED

not meant to remain in suspended animation.

I wish my non-affirming friends would come back to the conversation. There is much to say about the topic of truth. I find this a fascinating lesson of the Bible: put your ideas to the test! I believe there are five such tests: reason, the Bible, Spirit, tradition, and experience.

In our globally connected world of instant social media connections, our ideas will indeed be put to the test whether we like it or not. Our thoughts and words will be spun around the globe in an instant. Now more than ever we need deep thinkers and philosophical sages who test their ideas before spewing out careless words. We who affirm our LGBTQ friends and family do indeed have tough questions—questions I claim have answers. Are we rejecting the Bible? Can we live with our conscience? Do our conclusions pass the test? This is what Paul the Apostle is concerned with when he steps out onto theological waters and claims uncircumcised believers are in fact full-fledged believers. He wants to make sure he is not running in vain, as he puts it. And so Paul submits his idea to five tests—the idea that circumcision, though mandated by God's law, is no longer necessary for Christianity. Paul urges Christians to affirm uncircumcised believers as full-fledged Christians.

***Bible.*** Paul appeals to his "Bible", i.e. Scripture. Paul accepts that his point directly contradicts the law of God. "And the Scripture, foreseeing that God would justify the Gentiles by faith, preached the gospel beforehand to Abraham, saying, 'In you shall all the nations be blessed.'" (Galatians 3:8) Even though the written law of God says believers must be circumcised (Leviticus 12:2-3), Paul looks for hermeneutically illuminating verses in the sacred text. Paul willingly builds his theology on ideas contrary to the literal law of God, because he roots his theology in the hope of God that preceded the law given to Moses.

***Reason.*** Paul appeals to reason, to accepted principles about justification common to his audience at the time. He rebukes

Peter openly and sternly: "We who are Jews by birth and not sinful Gentiles know that a person is not justified by the works of the law, but by faith in Jesus Christ. So we, too, have put our faith in Christ Jesus that we may be justified by faith in Christ and not by the works of the law, because by the works of the law no one will be justified." (Galatians 2:15-16)

*Tradition.* Paul continued testing his idea about affirming the uncircumcised Gentiles by looking to tradition, the tradition of Abraham. Are Abraham's blessings, which preceded the law, reserved only for those who are circumcised? Might not the uncircumcised also share in these traditional blessings? "Christ redeemed us from the curse of the law by becoming a curse for us—for it is written, 'Cursed is everyone who is hanged on a tree'—so that in Christ Jesus the blessing of Abraham might come to the Gentiles, so that we might receive the promised Spirit through faith." (Galatians 3:13-14)

*Spirit.* Paul appeals to the Holy Spirit to make his point even more clear. "What I am saying is that as long as an heir is underage, he is no different from a slave, although he owns the whole estate. The heir is subject to guardians and trustees until the time set by his father. So also, when we were underage, we were in slavery under the elemental spiritual forces of the world. But when the set time had fully come, God sent his Son, born of a woman, born under the law, to redeem those under the law, that we might receive adoption to sonship. Because you are his sons, God sent the Spirit of his Son into our hearts, the Spirit who calls out, "Abba, Father." So you are no longer a slave, but God's child; and since you are his child, God has made you also an heir." (Galatians 4:1-7)

*Experience.* Paul makes an impressive concluding point about affirming the uncircumcised by urging his readers to look to the fruit they are experiencing. Are they seeing uncircumcised Christians indulging in wickedness? Or do the experience good fruit? By rejecting the uncircumcised, what kind of fruit are the law-enforcing Christians producing? "But the fruit of the Spirit is love, joy, peace, forbearance, kindness, goodness, faithfulness, gentleness and self-control. Against such things, there is no law. Those who belong to Christ Jesus have crucified the flesh with its passions and desires. Since we live by the Spirit, let us keep in step with the Spirit. Let us not become conceited, provoking and envying each other." (Galatians 5:22-26)

## BIBLE

As with many issues and debates, the church is left with a need to revisit the Bible and to find wisdom and insight from other sources. Never before has the guidance of the Holy Spirit been so needed. Yet, we have already followed the Spirit's guidance, learned from new knowledge gained outside the church, and revisited the Bible with all sorts of issues. At one time, left-handed people were excluded and looked down upon because they were thought to have some disorder that prevented them from conforming to God's right-handed design as found in the Bible. However, the church revisited the Bible. At one time, diseases like polio were thought to be the devil's curse. However, the church revisited the Bible. At one time, the earth was thought to be a fixed planet in space, and that the sun rotated around the earth. However, the church revisited the Bible.

Men and women who saw such things differently were deemed disobedient to the Bible and were often murdered as heretics. For example, the church rejected Galileo and his discoveries. Then it took more than 350 years for the church to officially apologize. My hope is that the church will become far swifter at apologies and much better at revisiting the Bible. Will the American church be able to use deeper discernment in our interactions with LGBTQ friends and family? I say we can. To do this, I suggest we shine light on Bible passages in new ways, all the while respecting the tradition and conscience of both affirming and non-affirming believers.

As I sift through the last five years of online and in-person discussions, debates, arguments, training and research, I am repeatedly drawn to the book of Galatians, Ephesians, and Hebrews. I am convinced that Galatians shows us the new wine Jesus promised, and that the book of Galatians in the Bible, like none other, has the effervescent power to spark reformation after reformation for the glory of God.

As a Christian who affirms the validity and sanctity of same-sex marriage and the full human legitimacy of our LGBTQ friends and family, I do not throw out the Bible. I have, however, adjusted my view of the Bible. In the Evangelical world where part of my prior theology is partially rooted, the idea is that all reason is to be justified by the Bible. The view is that the Bible contains all truth, and nothing but the truth. Conversations are allowed to end with the all-surpassing thought that "the Bible says it, so I believe it!" The idea is that no more reasoning is warranted when the Bible makes some kind of statement. This kind of theology is what I now reject, not the Bible itself.

The idea that the Bible is the master guidebook for morality is deeply ingrained in American churches. Some preach openly the mandate of accepting the Bible as "God's personal love letter to you" or "The Bible is the operations manual for humanity". This has been preached in America so much that the Bible has become an idol, worshipped as much as or even more than God. I find this idolatry at the heart of nearly every non-affirming position brought forth by Christians. Reasonable, critical thinking people see right through this fake religion. The American church would be wise to listen to such people.

My contention is that I have not thrown out the Bible, but that I have embraced the Bible in a new way. No longer is the Bible my guidebook. No longer is the Bible my idol. No longer is the Bible equal to Jesus. When read in its entirety (as I have done twice), I find the Bible has safeguards against idolatry built into it. The writings called Galatians have perhaps the best example of how we ought to approach the sacred text.

# UNCIRCUMCISED

No longer is religion to be guided or controlled by a written holiness code! Paul even goes as far as saying, "no one who relies on the law is justified before God." (Galatians 3:11). After the events of the life and death of Jesus of Nazareth, relying on the law of God given to Moses is not merely unhealthy, such a reliance is a cursed way of life (Galatians 3:10-14). In another letter in the Bible, Paul writes extensively about his own obedience to the law of God. Paul is circumcised, of the tribe of Benjamin, and a Jew of Jews. Yet Paul writes again and again about not putting any confidence in the righteousness that comes from following the law of God, as a safeguard for those who believe in the message of Christ. Then Paul exclaims: "I consider them garbage" (Philippians 3:1-14) To translate this in an outlaw preacher kind of way, Paul is saying holiness codes are manure!

If the Bible is not a moral guidebook or manual for human behavior, then what is the Bible? Instead of a guidebook of holiness, the Bible is a framework of reference. A main component of the new wine gospel message Jesus preached is that we no longer need a guardian of morality in written form. Paul's concluding remarks in Galatians 3:24-25 say this eloquently: "Before the coming of this faith, we were held in custody under the law, locked up until the faith that was to come would be revealed. So the law was our guardian until Christ came that we might be justified by faith. Now that this faith has come, we are no longer under a guardian."

What, then, is our guide for Christianity, if not the written law of God? My answer is again Paul's answer. Our guide is faith expressing itself through love (Galatians 5:6). Instead of treating human beings as machines who need an operating manual, Paul urges us to treat humanity with love. Whatever we believe from the Bible needs to be filtered through love.

# REASON

I find taking a time-out from the Bible to be deeply healing and highly restorative. Historical perspective is not only helpful, but also required, when discussing the challenges our LGBTQ friends and family face. Could we not reason our way through hostility with a better understanding of history? I find the following events from the past 500+ years to be fascinatingly relevant to the so-called gay debates.

## 1483

The Spanish Inquisition begins and includes imprisonment of men deemed to be gay, along with holy crusades to enforce moral conformity.

## 1485

The massive work, *Summa Theologica*, by Aquinas is published by the Holy See (Catholic publishing) and the church is infused with 3,000 pages of moral codes.

## 1517

Martin Luther nails his 95 grievances to the door of Wittenberg Castle church, Germany.

## 1532

The Holy Roman Empire institutes "sodomy" laws with the death penalty.

## 1661

American colonies outlaw "sodomy" and institute death penalty.

# UNCIRCUMCISED

## 1791

France becomes first Western country to decriminalize "sodomy".

## 1896

Sigmund Freud publishes works describing psychoanalysis and sees "sodomy" as a disorder.

## 1917

The United States medical association begins a uniform classification of disorders called the Diagnostic and Statistical Manual of Mental Disorders (DSM).

## 1922

The USSR (Soviets) decriminalize homosexual acts

## 1933

The German Nazi party begins persecution of homosexuals.

## 1946

The word "homosexuality" begins to be added to the Bible.

## 1947

*Summa Theologica* by Aquinas translated to English by The Fathers of the English Dominican Province.

## 1961

All US states continue to have sodomy laws. Some of these laws are a felony punishable by prison or hard labor.

## 1962

The American Law Institute creates the Model Penal Code to reduce the US sodomy laws.

## 1967

Homosexuality is decriminalized in England.

## 1972

The American Psychiatric Association declassifies homosexuality as a mental disorder.

## 1980'S

The AIDS tragedies begin. The US President, Ronald Reagan, remains silent.

# UNCIRCUMCISED

## 1990

The World Health Organization declassifies homosexuality as a mental disorder.

## 2003

The United States Supreme Court invalidates sodomy laws in the final 14 states.

## 2005

Canada legalizes same sex marriage.

## 2015

America legalizes same sex marriage.

## 2016

72 countries still have legal punishments by death or by prison or by hard labor around the world.

Such a timeline is sobering to me. While the church argues about theology, people are dying, being imprisoned, and being killed.

In addition to history, reason requires us to gain some understanding of medical science is necessary in order to affirm LGBTQ people. A severe lack of medical understanding has hindered not only LGBTQ people, but women as well, for centuries. Only in the late 1800's did we learn that the human body grows from the female egg. Until that time, the prevailing thought was that the woman was merely an incubator, and the entirety of human life came from the male sperm.

Understanding LGBTQ issues takes time—time our friends and family don't have. Still, I urge the church to learn about such things. Here is what I've learned so far (there is much more to learn here!)

Human sexuality is composed of at least four components: gender identity, gender expression, biological creation, and attraction orientation. None of these components, we are discovering, is binary in nature. Rather, the components of human sexuality are on a gradient. What is more, some of the components appear to be unchangeable for most; other components are fluid for others.

## GENDER IDENTITY SCALE

[woman, queer, man]

*How we identify our self; gender thinking*

## GENDER EXPRESSION SCALE

[feminine, neutral, masculine]

*How we dress, how we act, our mannerisms, etc.*

## BIOLOGICAL CREATION SCALE

[female, intersex, male]

*What body parts we have*

## ATTRACTION ORIENTATION SCALE

[women, both, male]

*Who we are attracted to*

The time for reasonable discussion is now. People are being mistreated, imprisoned, and killed.

# UNCIRCUMCISED TRADITION

The Christian church, as I observe it, has often fallen into the trap of developing disgust for things outside the currently defined boundaries of Christian community. Although the idea of an isolated community with an ideal communal morality is antithetical to what I see Jesus himself teaching in the Bible, Christians in many centuries have dug in their heels and formed such communities. The idea taught by Jesus is overwhelmingly obvious: love the other person, whether it is your neighbor, your enemy, the outcast, the poor, your fellow Christian, or even yourself. While millions of Christians have done amazing work to do just that—love the other—many more have rejected this critical tenet of Christianity.

Often, the Christian church struggles to welcome this "other" generation after generation. Instead of loving those in the margins of society, many Christians become known for whom they exclude from fellowship. This isolationist mentality took root right from the beginning in the first century Christian church. Each generation of Christians seems to find the idea of loving your neighbor to be a struggle and instead develops an elitist attitude, failing to heed Jesus' warning about yeast spreading through dough.

I contend that we are seeing three reformations that are challenging church traditions:

1. The disarming of religious authorities
2. The unleashing of freedoms of all kinds
3. The deconstruction of male-dominated patriarchy

These reformations are in fact rooted in Galatians (Galatians 3:28). In our divided world, I see these major divisions. Religious status division, social status division, and gender status division fragment both religious and secular communities.

In Galatians, Paul writes about the division between Jew and Greek. The circumcision party was very much in control until Peter and Paul resolved the tension and found the way through their religious division. Tradition said only circumcised people could partake of God's blessings. However, Paul found God was doing a new thing—uncircumcised Christians were equally blessed and equally charged with leadership in the church.

The early Christians came to realize their uncircumcised family, friends, and neighbors were full-fledged Christians and did not need to become circumcised to fit into the Christian church. This transformation, I believe, was made possible by Christians such as Paul who revisited the sacred Scriptures and challenged the longstanding traditions of the religion around him.

## SPIRIT

The cliché question hip Christians sometimes ask me during the LGBTQ theology debates is, "What would Jesus do?" I do not presume to know what Jesus would do. I can guess it would be stunning and unexpected. The better, more helpful question is, "What did Jesus do?" When we examine what Jesus is recorded as doing instead of surmising what Jesus might do, we find some curious and relevant actions. For example, Jesus associated with the wrong people. Jesus let himself be unclean by touching a leper. Jesus earned the labels of glutton and a drunkard by his unorthodox disciple-making methods. This Spirit of Jesus is a fascinating guide to our interactions with LGBTQ people.

The Spirit of Jesus is revealed strikingly in the Bible story about the woman at Jacob's well (John 4). By both religious and social moral standards, this woman was an immoral woman.

> "A woman from Samaria came to draw water. Jesus said to her, "Give me a drink." (For his disciples had gone away into the city to buy food.) The Samaritan woman said to him, "How is it that you, a Jew, ask for a drink from me, a woman of Samaria?" (For Jews have no dealings with Samaritans.)

# UNCIRCUMCISED

*Jesus answered her, "If you knew the gift of God, and who it is that is saying to you, 'Give me a drink,' you would have asked him, and he would have given you living water." (John 4:7-10)*

I find little difference between this woman at the well and another woman Jesus encountered—the woman caught in adultery. To one woman, Jesus said, "Go and sin no more!" To the other, Jesus made no mention of sin (although Jesus did touch on the subject when he later asked her to call her husband). In this story, Jesus shared the gospel with the immoral woman but did not exclude her because of her situation. At the end of this story, the woman has renewed interest in Jesus and sees him as the Messiah, but she would still be considered immoral by her community—she was still living with her boyfriend. This fact does not bother Jesus, and he does not change her living arrangements.

This is the Spirit of Jesus—to befriend the outcast, to share good news, to welcome and to affirm without condemning.

## EXPERIENCE

In the final analysis, I suspect no theology will change any Christian's mind. It is the experience of interacting with LGBTQ people that so often opens people's minds and hearts. It is the experience of interacting with non-affirming Christians that convicts the minds of affirming Christians. I believe this is why Jesus embedded the wisdom of inclusion in his teaching and ministry. Railing against same-sex marriage or transgender rights or your conservative Christian friend on social media may be a heart-racing infusion of self-righteousness, but shock jolts through your veins when you realize your own son, daughter, friend, cousin, aunt, or parent is at the other end of your attack. Such experiences are becoming the norm, and much healing is going to be needed in the coming years. Will the church be there to aid in this healing process?

What will happen when we welcome our LGBTQ family and friends to the Christian table? What will change when the church affirms LGBTQ people for who they are? What will the church become when we give all people, straight or otherwise, the freedom to figure out their sexuality?

Some pastors paint a dark picture of sin sweeping through the church like a tsunami. Other pastors weep for America who is supposedly betraying our God. I see such foreboding thoughts, however, primarily stemming from a flawed understanding of holiness. If such pastors really see LGBTQ as so sinful and unholy, then they ought to be swimming out into that tsunami to help them.

I see a much brighter and far more glorious picture of what LGBTQ people might bring to the church! Such people will bring at least three gifts to the church, gifts that are sorely needed. They bring the gift of heart, and will move the Christian church toward courage, hope, and compassion. They bring the gift of holiness, and will challenge the church to rethink holiness, dig deeper, and find a better sense of conscience and purity. And perhaps needed more than any gift, our LGBTQ friends and family will bring the gift of celebration! My times of worship and Bible study with LGBTQ people have been times of all-surpassing joy, remarkable hospitality, and amazing fellowship.

In addition to various gifts, I see LGBTQ people bringing major corrections to Christian theology. They challenge Christians to find a more robust understanding of the gospel, to move beyond atonement toward reconciliation, and to revisit the Bible we think we know so well. They will bring a restoration to the purpose of the church. Are we sin police? Who is King? Who is Lord? In time, we will discover that Christian churches are not to be army battalions fighting sin, but hospitals healing the people. Our LGBTQ family and friends will bring with them an excitement about philosophy and life itself! The passion and enthusiasm of gender and sexual outliers that stems from being both welcomed and affirmed is electrifying.

In the end, I see epoch-level reformation and transformation for the church worldwide, not seen since Calvin and Luther 500 years ago, when we affirm LGBTQ people. Finally, perhaps, we will see God's vision of inclusion and love for all people.

## NO FEAR

Where does truth lead? Truth is often a fearful subject, and typically missing from the conversations on LGBTQ topics. When truth is brought into the discussion, truth is used as a fear-inducing tool, perhaps meant to scare away the gay.

Fear is a complicated subject in the Bible. The direction to "be not afraid" is indeed the most often repeated command in the Bible text. Yet there are places where we are admonished to "fear him who, after he has killed, has authority to cast into hell." (Luke 12:5). My point here is not to expound on the topic of fear and all its nuances. My point is the conclusion: there is no fear in love. In the end, the Bible directs us to love without fear. Ponder these amazing thoughts…

> "There is no fear in love, but perfect love casts out fear. For fear has to do with punishment, and whoever fears has not been perfected in love. We love because he first loved us. If anyone says, "I love God," and hates his brother, he is a liar; for he who does not love his brother whom he has seen cannot love God whom he has not seen. And this commandment we have from him: whoever loves God must also love his brother." (1 John 4:18-21)

I am bound to love, and love is a far fiercer master than the law. Love demands that I act kindly toward my non-affirming friends and family, but I have not always done so. Love demands that I forgive those who have enacted much abuse, but I have not always done so. Love demands that I do not hate my LGBTQ friends and family, but I have not always done so.

The fact that some of the greatest theologians of our time cannot come up with anything better than "cry together" as a direction for the church speaks volumes to the complex and taboo nature of Christians welcoming our LGBTQ friends and family. Yet, I contend that such a welcome ought to be as simple as a child who loves his mother or a mother who loves her child.

I intend to continue this walk through the door of affirmation, to discover the hermeneutically illuminating verses in the Bible, to repeatedly extol the Christian experiences of LGBTQ people, and to urge the American Christian church to dissolve the wall of hostility by fully affirming our LGBTQ friends and family. My prayer is that the 21st century church may offer the right hand of fellowship to LGBTQ people and their allies, just as the first century church welcomed the uncircumcised.

> *"...and when James and Cephas and John, who seemed to be pillars, perceived the grace that was given to me, they gave the right hand of fellowship to Barnabas and me, that we should go to the Gentiles and they to the circumcised."*
>
> *- Galatians 2:9*

*other books by*
## BRIAN JOHN KARCHER

---

## EVIL
*Confronting our Inner Hitler*

## THE LAMBHEARTED LION
*Why Christianity needs Gay People*

## IDENTITY SNATCHERS
*Exposing a Korean Campus Bible Cult*

*Available online at*
## AMAZON
*and other retailers worldwide*

# ABOUT THE AUTHOR

Brian John Karcher is a Christ-follower on the journey of life who loves family, friends, philosophy, writing, blogging and dialogue. He is a computer engineer who recently stepped into the path of leadership. He is happily married to Dr. Mary since 1994 and has four amazing children.

Brian's religious background is extensive. He grew up in the Roman Catholic Church and at one time considered becoming a priest. In college, Brian became a leader in a campus bible study organization from Korea where he donated nearly 40 hours of time every week for 16 years. He has gone to Russia as a missionary, amassed over 20,000 hours of bible meditation and was "pastor" in his own house church for eight years. In 2012 he was baptized at a local North American Baptist church.

After leaving college ministry, Brian has participated in a VantagePoint3 Journey Cohort in 2013, an ACT3 Missional Ecumenical Leadership Cohort in 2014, and Matthew Vine's Reformation Project Leadership Cohort in Washington D.C. in 2015.

*Yacoub & Tomás*

www.ingramcontent.com/pod-product-compliance
Lightning Source LLC
Chambersburg PA
CBHW050542300426
44113CB00012B/2231